THE EVENT-DRIVEN EDGE IN INVESTING

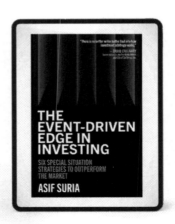

THE EVENT-DRIVEN EDGE IN INVESTING

Six Special Situation Strategies to Outperform the Market

ASIF SURIA

HARRIMAN HOUSE LTD
3 Viceroy Court
Bedford Road
Petersfield
Hampshire
GU32 3LJ
GREAT BRITAIN
Tel: +44 (0)1730 233870

Email: enquiries@harriman-house.com
Website: harriman.house

First published in 2024.

Hardback ISBN: 978-1-80409-080-0
Paperback ISBN: 978-1-80409-049-7
eBook ISBN: 978-1-80409-050-3

British Library Cataloguing in Publication Data

A CIP catalogue record for this book can be obtained from the British Library.

Dedicated to the bright shining STAR in my life.

CONTENTS

PREFACE

IDEA GENERATION IS the lifeblood of investors. I am constantly looking at new investment opportunities and end up investing in a very small fraction of the ideas I explore. If most of my investing ideas are generated from the same sources that millions of other investors rely on, then my investment performance is likely to be mediocre. I would be better off investing in a broadly diversified index like the S&P 500 Index, which includes the 500 largest companies in the United States.

Event-driven investing, as the name implies, involves investing in companies that are experiencing a specific event. These events can have a transformative impact on the company and can range from the company spinning off a division into a separate public company to merging with another company. You can be successful using these strategies without the need to predict earnings or the short-term direction of the market.

I was drawn to event-driven investing because it introduced me to strategies that were a source of fresh investment ideas. As an added cherry on the top, certain event-driven strategies also perform well during times of market distress.

This book is for both self-directed investors and professional investors that are looking for alternative strategies to complement their current investment process, as sources of idea generation and to benefit from the positive market reaction to transformative events.

This book explores six different event-driven strategies in detail. I will walk you through the nuances of each strategy and outline how these strategies will help you navigate the ups and downs of financial markets. Some strategies work well during declining market environments, while others are an excellent way to make money coming out of a bear market.

After a general introduction of these six event-driven strategies, I will use case studies in each chapter and delve into the specifics of how each strategy works. I briefly discuss instruments like options, futures, and bonds to whet your appetite about them and describe the interplay of these instruments with certain event-driven strategies.

Understanding when a strategy does not work is just as important as figuring out the upside it offers. I explore the pitfalls of each strategy and what to avoid in a "dark side" section in each strategy chapter.

The strategies discussed in the book include legal insider transactions, merger arbitrage, stock buybacks, SPACs, spinoffs and management changes.

INTRODUCTION

IN A 2017 interview, Charlie Munger, the vice-chairman of Berkshire Hathaway and Warren Buffett's investing partner, recounted how he made $80 million risk-free from an idea he came across in the weekly financial magazine *Barron's*.

"I read *Barron's* for 50 years. In 50 years I found one investment opportunity in *Barron's* out of which I made about $80 million with almost no risk. I took the $80 million and gave it to Li Lu who turned it into $400 or $500 million. So I have made $400 or $500 million from reading *Barron's* for 50 years and following one idea."

When I first started investing, I followed the same sources for idea generation as most other investors. I read financial magazines like *Barron's* and *Fortune*, talked to other investors, ran stock screens and used investment-focused websites.

I came across one of my more successful investment ideas, Twilio, from an article in *Fortune* magazine about the founder of the company, Jeff Lawson. Twilio makes it very easy for companies to send text messages to their customers without having to deal with the complexities of delivering messages to different mobile phone networks in multiple countries. If you have used Uber, it is likely that the message notifying you that your driver or food order has arrived was facilitated by Twilio.

The article about Twilio in *Fortune* was written before the company went public, and something about the way Mr. Lawson managed the company stayed in the back of my mind. A few months later, Twilio went public in an initial public offering (IPO) priced at $15 per share, and the stock soared 92% on its first day of trading. When Twilio's stock started declining following the usual IPO-related pop in its stock price, I decided to buy Twilio and watched the stock go up more than 1,600%. It also helped that Mr. Lawson purchased shares on the open market at the same time.

I had been reading *Fortune* for well over a decade before I came across Twilio. One decade of reading for one profitable idea. The legal insider purchase by the CEO was the catalyst that led to my purchase of Twilio.

I started my investing journey during the depths of the bear market that followed the dot-com bubble in 2000. To be precise, I started investing during the bear market rally that began in April 2001 and lasted a few weeks. During a bear market rally, stocks rise sharply in a temporary respite from the incessant selling that precedes them.

I got off to a great start. I was following a simple momentum strategy and managed to generate returns of over 30% in a few weeks. Those returns were beginner's luck. I had not done in-depth research on momentum strategies and all I was doing was speculating on stocks that had shown strength and kept going up for a period of time.

After I had generated those quick 30% returns, I started thinking that the strategy I was using was so rudimentary that it was bound to falter sooner rather than later. Listening to the wise counsel of investors that were more experienced than me, I decided to look for a safe blue-chip company for my next investment; preferably one that was trading at a discount to its intrinsic value.

A safe blue-chip investment?

The company I picked happened to be the seventh largest company in the U.S. and the largest energy-trading company in the world. As an added bonus, it had seen its stock cut in half in recent months. The new CEO of the company was encouraging employees to buy shares, indicated the company was doing well, and predicted a "significantly higher stock price."

Each of these things would have been big red flags for experienced investors: A stock that has declined rapidly, a company in a cyclical industry during a recession, and the CEO cheering the stock on. Unfortunately, there was still a lot of learning I had to do as a novice investor.

The company I picked was none other than Enron. I bought it at around $30 per share. Two months after I purchased shares, Enron reported a large quarterly loss and the U.S. Securities and Exchange Commission (SEC) opened an investigation.

It turned out that Enron was an accounting fraud and had been using accounting tricks to make its results look much better than they actually were.

As the huge fraud at Enron unfolded and the stock dropped from $30 to $10, I asked other investors who had been investing for longer than I had whether I should cut my losses and sell. The advice I received was to stay the course. Investors and traders are often an optimistic bunch. They find it hard to admit a mistake and take a quick loss. I was no different and rode that "investment" all the way down from $30 to 30 cents. I eventually sold right before the company declared bankruptcy, taking a 99% loss. Taking a loss quickly and avoiding an even larger one down the road is an investing superpower that few investors are able to harness consistently.

Learning about investing

I was fortunate to have encountered this Enron debacle early in my investing journey. My portfolio was small, I had no leverage, I had a job I loved, and I did not have a family to support. The experience was, however, painful enough to get me started down the path of learning the art and science of investing. I taught myself to read financial statements, picked up books by the investment gurus Benjamin Graham, Philip Fisher, and Peter Lynch, and started to understand comparative valuation metrics like Price/Earnings and Price/Tangible Book ratios. The book *Hedgehogging* by Barton Biggs helped me understand how sentiment and investor psychology played a big role in short-term market movements.[1]

As time progressed, I learned from the school of hard knocks and from other investors that were on a similar journey. I started writing an investment blog in 2005 and the writing process helped me delve into broader topics like asset allocation, position sizing, and how to estimate the intrinsic value of a company by building a discounted cash flow (DCF) model.

Towards the end of 2005, I reached out to the CEO of an emerging investment website called Seeking Alpha. After reading my content, he agreed to start publishing my blog on Seeking Alpha. As an early contributor, I was able to interact with retail and institutional investors that were using the website.

My introduction to event-driven investing

A hedge fund manager who had been reading my articles reached out to me in 2010 to discuss a special situation where a company that was in the process of getting acquired by another company was trading well below the acquisition price.

The hedge fund manager told me that all I had to do was buy the target company, wait for the merger to close, and pocket the difference between the current price and the acquisition price. This strategy is referred to as merger arbitrage and it is one of the strategies that I introduce to you later in this book. I had been introduced to the merger arbitrage strategy several years before this interaction with the hedge fund manager, but the discussion with him helped me start on a long journey towards understanding, tracking, and benefiting from event-driven investing.

I started tracking two event-driven strategies—legal insider transactions and merger arbitrage—in 2010 on two different websites, which I later combined into InsideArbitrage.com in 2018.

Writing consistently can be a reward in itself. It helps distill your thought process, dive deeper into topics and learn from interactions with your audience. Another added benefit is that you get to meet people you would not have expected to meet otherwise. The author and investor Morgan Housel was surprised to learn that Bill Gates was reading his work based on a tweet by the founder of Microsoft. This was many years before Morgan Housel went on to write the immensely successful book *The Psychology of Money*.

A venture capitalist out of Seattle who was interested in legal insider transactions and who had been reading my work reached out to me. After we got to know each other, we decided to team up to do in-depth research on insider transactions using a combination of traditional data analysis techniques and machine learning. Using more than a decade of insider transactions and several decades of fundamental data from FactSet, we were thrilled to find a series of algorithmic trading strategies that outperformed the market in our backtests.

Registering as advisors in the states of California and Washington, we raised an experimental seed fund to test our strategies with real money. We then built software that would automatically trade for us, creating an end-to-end automated process where the algorithm picked the investments, purchased the stock for us and then sold it at the end of our holding period. Our first year of running this experiment worked out great, with returns of 23% that beat our benchmark index. Unfortunately, as is often the case with data-driven processes, we attempted to optimize the strategy further by overlaying a value-oriented framework just as value stocks started significantly underperforming growth stocks. The underperformance persisted for years. Instead of raising a larger fund, we decided to wind down our experimental fund.

Six event-driven strategies

I learned several valuable lessons from the experience and decided to expand my framework to include six different event-driven strategies. These strategies became an integral part of my portfolio management process, both in terms of idea generation and to generate returns that were uncorrelated with the market. When the markets zig, some of these strategies zag. Although I must add that at times of extreme market stress most asset classes tend to become correlated and move in unison.

As described earlier, event-driven investing involves investing in companies that are experiencing a specific event.

The big advantage of event-driven strategies is that they allow you to have a flexible mental model of investing. You can be nimble and adopt a strategy that works for the current market environment instead of remaining pigeonholed into a certain investing style that may not work for an extended period of time.

In some cases, these strategies also provide a macro-signal, letting you know that the market may be at an inflection point. I've seen this multiple times with unusually strong insider buying near the end of a bear market, as discussed in the insider transactions chapter in this book.

A third advantage is that you start seeing patterns. The same companies start bubbling up across strategies. Insiders of a company might be buying shares even as the company is buying back its own stock. In one instance, I found a company attractive because it was in the process of getting acquired and was planning on spinning off a division as an independent company post-acquisition. Both the acquisition and the spinoff provided opportunities and it was encouraging to see that an insider was also buying stock right before the acquisition closed. I discuss this situation in more detail as a case study in the Spinoff chapter later in the book.

This trifecta of idea generation, macro-signals and unique patterns that emerge from following these strategies has been very powerful in helping me construct and manage portfolios.

While this book does not explore every event-driven or special situations strategy, it provides a comprehensive overview of six strategies that are accessible to both retail and professional investors and will help expand your investing toolbox to handle different market environments.

Let's move on to Chapter 1, where I provide a brief background to the strategies discussed in this book.

CHAPTER 1

EVENT-DRIVEN STRATEGIES

 Merger Arbitrage   Spinoffs   Stock Buybacks

 Insider Transactions   SPACS   C-Suite Transitions

Event-driven investing, sometimes also known as special situations investing, encompasses a wide range of individual strategies that have one thing in common: they usually involve a significant event that changes the nature or trajectory of a business.

A good example is mergers and acquisitions (M&A). A merger or an acquisition can have a large impact on both the target and the acquiring company, and a strategy related to M&A fits within the realm of event-driven investing.

Similarly, a company spinning off a division into a separate independent company is called a spinoff. The global consulting company Accenture was spun out of one of the largest accounting firms, Arthur Andersen, in 2001. This spinoff was timely, as less than a year later, Arthur Andersen was convicted of obstruction of justice. The charge stemmed from Arthur Andersen's role as Enron's auditor, where they helped Enron doctor certain documents and assisted with the shredding of documents. Shortly after the conviction, the 89-year-old Arthur Andersen ceased to exist, while the spinoff Accenture continued to thrive and became a company worth over $160 billion.

In this chapter, I provide a quick introduction to each of the six event-driven strategies I cover in this book. These are:

Merger arbitrage

Insider transactions

Stock buybacks

SPACS

Spinoffs

Management changes

Each subsequent chapter is then dedicated to one event-driven strategy.

Merger arbitrage

When two companies decide to merge or when a large company announces the acquisition of a smaller one, the target company rarely trades at the agreed acquisition price. In most instances, it trades a little below the acquisition price. In some instances, where there is significant uncertainty about whether the deal will close or not, the target company might trade at a large discount to the acquisition price.

The strategy of buying a target company at a discount and waiting for the deal to close in order to pick up the difference between the current market price and the acquisition price is called merger arbitrage. This difference between the current price and the acquisition price is called the spread.

The strategy is also known as risk arbitrage because investors that use this strategy are taking on the risk that the deal might not close and the stock might drop sharply to pre-deal levels. In return for taking this risk, they pick up a few pennies or dollars in a trade that has a high probability of closing.

Considering investors are only getting paid a few pennies, for the strategy to work, most deals have to close. I analyzed over 12 years of deal data from 2010 to 2022 and it was encouraging to see that 95% of announced deals close.

An example of a deal with a small spread was Berkshire Hathaway's acquisition of the insurance company Alleghany for $848.02 per share, which was announced on March 31, 2022. By September 30, 2022, the stock was trading at $840.56. The spread on the deal was $7.46, or less than 1% of the purchase price. An arbitrageur would have captured this $7.46 per share profit when the deal closed on October 19, 2022.

In case you are wondering why the acquisition price is $848.02 and not $848 or even $850, there is an interesting little story behind that $848.02 number. Warren Buffett is famously averse to paying fees to middlemen. He likes to deal directly with companies when he acquires them for Berkshire Hathaway and prefers not to have investment bankers involved. There was a time in 1986 when he issued a full-page ad in the *Wall Street Journal* looking for companies worth $100 million or more that were willing to sell themselves.

In the case of Alleghany, he offered to buy the company for $850 per share but did not want to pay the fees of investment bankers. The final price of $848.02 reflects the exclusion of the financial advisory fee that has to be paid to the investment banks associated with the deal.

On the other end of the spectrum from the Alleghany deal was the acquisition of Twitter by Elon Musk. The deal had more twists and turns than a well-executed murder mystery. At one point in the saga, on July 11, 2022, the merger arbitrage situation offered a potential profit or spread of 66%.

In the merger arbitrage chapter, I explore why there was a significant difference in the spreads of these two deals, various deal types, and how you can use this strategy in your portfolio, especially during challenging market conditions.

Insider transactions

Investors in public companies usually have limited information about the companies they are invested in. They get periodic updates through quarterly earnings calls and SEC filings. In some instances, they might get to watch a management presentation mid-quarter at an investor conference, or if they have a large enough stake in the company they may get to talk to management.

In contrast, insiders of the company have full visibility into what is happening at the current moment, how the business's product pipeline is evolving, and the progress on large contracts that might be on the horizon. Clearly, insiders have an information advantage compared to public market investors.

Company insiders, including members of the management team like the CEO and the CFO, can purchase and sell shares of their company on the open market. When they complete a purchase or a sale, they are required to report this insider transaction to the SEC within two business days. Investors watch these transactions closely to understand the sentiment of the company's insiders and determine if the insider transactions signal potential opportunity or trouble for the stock.

Insider transactions don't normally fall into the realm of event-driven strategies because they are not events that can have a transformative impact on a company. However, the signals insider transactions provide can indicate that a stock is materially cheap or expensive, justifying the strategy's inclusion with the other event-driven strategies discussed in this book.

Stock buybacks

We are all attracted to bargains and like to buy things when they are on sale at a significant discount. Companies and their insiders are no different. When they notice that the market, during temporary bouts of euphoria, has bid up the price of their stock to levels that are not supported by the fundamentals of the company, they tend to sell shares. Insiders sell shares on the open market and companies sell additional shares to investors through what is called a secondary offering.

Every time a company offers shares to the investing public after its initial public offering (IPO), it is called a secondary offering, even if it has offered shares to the public on a second, third, fourth, etc., occasion in the past. Terms like tertiary offering, quaternary offering, quinary offering, etc. are not used, and I don't blame them because some companies issue new shares over and over again, so the terminology would get out of hand.

The money generated from secondary offerings could be used to expand the current business, enter a new line of business, or acquire other companies for cash.

The impact for existing shareholders is that a secondary offering dilutes their existing stake in the business and secondary offerings often lead to a temporary drop in the stock price.

Companies pay heed to Warren Buffett's advice to be "fearful when others are greedy, and greedy when others are fearful". They not only issue new shares when the stock is expensive; they also tend to buy shares from the open market or directly from investors when they think the stock is cheap.

During market downturns and turmoil, smart management teams and their board of directors decide to repurchase shares and reduce their share count. William Thorndike's book *The Outsiders* attempted to identify why some CEOs were more successful than others.[2] In many cases, it boiled down to their capital allocation decisions and specifically when to issue more shares and when to repurchase them.

In the stock buybacks chapter, I discuss the difference between buyback announcements and actual purchases, as well as a screen that combines both insider buying and stock buybacks.

SPACS

In the year 2000, right after the dot-com bubble had burst, I came across two entrepreneurs from Chicago that had moved to the town of Eugene, Oregon to acquire a jewelry business. What was unique about them was that they had first raised a pool of capital from investors (about half a million dollars) and then went around looking for an operating business to buy with that money. They found a small jeweler in Oregon called Jody Coyote and decided to acquire the business.

While one partner focused on front-end business development by opening up access to large companies like Macy's (NYSE: M), the other one focused on back-end operations.

The business under their management went on to generate handsome returns for them and for their investors. The two entrepreneurs from Chicago, Chris Cunning and Peter Day, had inspired so much confidence in their investors that the investors were willing to write a check to the duo without knowing what kind of company they would eventually end up acquiring and growing. This was my introduction to what was back then called a "blank check company" and what is now known as a Special Purpose Acquisition Company (SPAC).

Investors that have access to large pools of money sometimes create SPACs that are usually seeded with several hundred million dollars worth of capital. Once this company is created and funded through an IPO, it begins a two-year search for a private operating company with a real business. If the SPAC manages to find an operating company it likes, the publicly traded SPAC merges with the private operating company. This process allows the private company to go public quickly through a simpler process compared to a traditional IPO. The folks that started the SPAC (the sponsors) benefit from getting a large stake in the combined company. Examples of companies that went public through a SPAC include the co-working company WeWork, the social network Nextdoor, and the fintech company SoFi.

What was previously a sleepy corner of capital markets entered into a huge bubble in 2020 and 2021 with hundreds of SPACs created.

If the SPAC does not find an operating business within its two-year lifespan, it has to return the money to its investors along with any interest collected on the money while it was sitting idle waiting for a suitor. This creates an incentive for the SPAC sponsor to find an operating company to merge with. Some of the businesses the 2020 and 2021 vintage SPACs merged with had little more than a business plan and no sales or profits. Companies that were not ready to go public took this easy route and their stocks inevitably collapsed post-merger.

The entire process generates several opportunities for investors to make money from SPACs and in some cases with minimal risk. In the chapter on SPACs I discuss the nuances of this strategy in detail and cover the various opportunities SPACs provide for investors.

Spinoffs

Every once in a while, we get a movie or TV franchise that is spun off from another movie and turns out to be more successful than the original. The rather amusing *Minions* was spun out of *Despicable Me* and *Deadpool* was spun out of *X-Men Origins: Wolverine*.

Corporate America has something similar, where entire companies suffer a repressed existence inside a large company and yearn to be free through a spinoff.

The movie *Ford v Ferrari* recounts how the Italian car powerhouse Fiat stole Ferrari from Ford. Ferrari had been negotiating with Ford to acquire the racing car company when Fiat swooped in at the last minute to walk away with the prize. Fiat went on to expand its ownership of Ferrari from 50% in 1969 to 90% by 1988. Ferrari lived under its corporate overlords for several decades before being ultimately spun off as a separate public company in 2015 with the clever stock symbol RACE.

After an initial drop and underperforming the S&P 500 for much of its first year as a public company, Ferrari raced higher and in its first five years managed to register gains of 237% compared to a gain of just 67% for the S&P 500.

This pattern of initial underperformance followed by subsequent outperformance is a feature and not a bug of spinoffs. When companies are spun out of their parents, large funds and professional investors often do not want to keep the spinoff in their portfolio and tend to sell them shortly after the separation. This creates temporary selling pressure and an opportunity for investors that are willing to ride out the near-term volatility.

I explore the different types of spinoffs and how to determine if the spinoff or the parent makes for a better investment in the spinoffs chapter of this book.

Management changes

When you hear the names Henry Ford, Mary Barra, Howard Schultz, Jeff Bezos, and Lee Kuan Yew, you are reminded of a founder who reshaped an industry, a CEO that rescued a behemoth from mediocrity, an entrepreneur that transformed how we consume coffee, a visionary leader that gave us the Everything Store, and a politician that put a tiny island nation on the map.

These leaders were innovative, they worked tirelessly, and they inspired their employees, fellow countrymen, and followers to create something special. We have seen time and again how companies falter and lose their way when their visionary founder CEO departs. This is one of the reasons Howard Schultz returned as CEO of Starbucks not once, but twice. The ranks of these so-called boomerang CEOs include Michael Dell of Dell, Steve Jobs of Apple, Jack Dorsey of Twitter, and many more.

William Ford Jr., the great grandson of both Henry Ford, the founder of Ford Motor Company, and Harvey Firestone, the founder of Firestone Tire and Rubber, served as Ford's CEO from 2001 to 2006. Realizing that he was better suited to being the Executive Chairman of the company, he poached Alan Mulally from Boeing to join Ford as its CEO in 2006. Mr. Mulally was instrumental in returning Ford to profitability and shepherded the company through the Great Recession, helping Ford avoid bankruptcy unlike the other big American car companies.

Given the disproportionate impact the leader at the top can have on an organization, it is important for investors to pay attention to management changes at their portfolio companies. A leader with a successful track record joining a company that is in trouble could also be a signal to investors.

The management changes chapter of this will book highlights signals from new appointments and red flags from management departures.

This concludes our short introduction to each of the event-driven strategies discussed in this book. We will now move on to taking a closer look at each strategy and explore them in more detail through various case studies.

CHAPTER 2

MERGER ARBITRAGE

IMAGINE A COUPLE about to exchange vows on their wedding day, when the priest utters the traditional words "speak now or forever hold your peace." Since the medieval period, when information didn't flow quite as freely as it does now, the church has included this phrase to allow any issues to come to light.

In most weddings no one raises an objection, and the marriage is allowed to proceed. The couple heads out with love in their hearts and hopes of a better future together.

Mergers and acquisitions in the corporate world are remarkably similar. Where two similar-sized companies merge with each other, this is known as a merger of equals; and when a large company like Google acquires a smaller company like the wearable device maker Fitbit, it is called an acquisition—although some investors, including yours truly, use the words "merger" and "acquisition" interchangeably. After a courtship period that is sometimes facilitated by investment bankers, and at other times happens shockingly fast over a single dinner, two companies decide to sign a definitive merger agreement. Then they start making plans for the big day, when their merger will be consummated.

The companies envision a better future together with "synergies" realized from combining their strengths and assets. Just like the aforementioned wedding, for the most part no one objects to the merger, and nearly 95% of announced mergers complete as expected. However, every once in a while, someone decides not to hold their peace and objects to the merger.

The spoilsport could be a government regulator concerned that the merger would leave consumers with fewer choices and the combined company with potentially monopolistic pricing power.

At other times it could be a dissenting shareholder who feels that their beloved company is being sold for a song and could do much better, translating to a higher share price for the shareholder.

In rare instances the acquiring person or company might realize they don't have the money needed to complete the merger, despite assurances by bankers or third parties that they will help finance the deal.

I cover all these killjoys later in this chapter. Suffice to say, there are hurdles companies face in completing mergers, and the potential risk of these hurdles provides a special group of investors an opportunity to benefit even after the deal is publicly announced.

This special group of investors are called arbitrageurs, and they step in to buy the stock of companies that are merging or one that is being acquired, from long-term investors, who might not want to wait around to see whether the merger actually closes or falls apart.

Before we can dive into the specifics of why arbitrageurs like to step in, let us first discuss arbitrage in a broader context.

Arbitrage

Arbitrage is an investment strategy in which a person buys an asset in one market and sells it at a higher price in another market to capture the price difference between the two markets. In its simplest form, the strategy expects nearly risk-free profits with minimal friction.

Saffron quality can vary significantly depending on where the saffron crocus flower from which it is extracted is grown, and the highest quality saffron in the world is grown on the high Castilian plateau known as La Mancha in Spain. For a simple example of arbitrage, consider the ability to buy high quality saffron from Spain and sell it across the Atlantic at a higher price in Québec City in Canada.

The friction in this arbitrage trade would be shipping costs and any potential damage to the goods in transit. Obviously the trader has precious capital tied up in the trade and is impacted both by supply and demand cycles and, most importantly, competition. If others got wind of the big price differential for saffron between La Mancha, Spain and Quebec City, they would start importing the same goods and the profits would shrink. In other words, as the investing crowd likes to say, the opportunity would be arbitraged away. In the global world we live in, spice traders of old have been arbitraged away and you can find La Mancha Saffron in both Walmart (NYSE: WMT) and Costco (NASDAQ: COST).

There are many forms of arbitrage that exist in financial markets. Certain companies could have their stock listed in multiple markets either within the same country or across countries. Arbitrageurs used to watch for price differentials and capture them by buying in one market and selling in another. Considering these price differentials were very small, friction in the form of trading costs and differences in currency rates (if trading across countries) could eat up some of the profits. In recent years, the same strategy was employed with cryptocurrency by buying bitcoin in one country and selling it in another that had greater demand and hence a higher price.

Other arbitrage opportunities include the difference in price between different classes of shares for the same stock. For example, Zillow has Class A shares (NASDAQ: ZG) and Class C shares (NASDAQ: Z) that often trade at different prices because of the difference in voting rights between those two classes of shares. Class A shares of Zillow give shareholders a vote, whether it is to elect new directors to the board or vote on an acquisition of the company. Class C shareholders get the same economic benefits from owning the stock as Class A shareholders but don't get to vote.

Other companies with multiple classes of shares include Heico (NYSE: HEI.A and NYSE: HEI), Lions Gate Entertainment (NYSE: LGF.A and NYSE: LGF.B) and the most famous of them all, Berkshire Hathaway (NYSE: BRK.A and NYSE: BRK.B). The difference in price might not always close unless there is a corporate event such as an acquisition of the company, the company decides to buy back a certain class of shares or the company uplists the stock from an over-the-counter (OTC) market to a major exchange like the NYSE.

The strangest case of dual class arbitrage I have seen occurred in mid-2023 with the regional bank First Citizens BancShares that had just acquired Silicon Valley Bank in a sweetheart deal brokered by the Federal Deposit Insurance Corps after Silicon Valley Bank failed. First Citizens' class B shares (OTC: FCNCB) were trading at a big discount to class A shares (NASDAQ: FCNCA). On June 23, 2023 class B shares of First Citizens were trading at $1,050 compared to class A shares that closed the day at $1,208. The strange part here was that each class B share of the company had 16 votes compared to one vote for each class A share. Normally the shares that have more votes or a greater claim to the company's profits through a higher dividend would trade at a premium to other classes of shares. The only logical explanation in this case was that class B shares were not listed on a major exchange like the NYSE and trading volume was low.

Closed-end funds arbitrage and statistical arbitrage (also called stat arb) are two additional strategies that sophisticated retail investors and professional investors employ. A closed-end fund is an investment company that raises a fixed amount of capital through an initial public offering (IPO) and then trades on an exchange like a stock. After the initial IPO, no more shares are normally issued by the fund. In mid-2023, there were approximately 480 closed-end funds trading on U.S. stock exchanges. Closed-end funds are actively managed and tend to charge higher fees than open-end funds or ETFs.

The market price of a closed-end fund's shares may differ from the value of its underlying assets (also called the Net Asset Value or NAV). If it trades above the NAV, it is said to be trading at a premium and if the market price is below its NAV, the fund is said to be at a discount. Discounts can widen significantly, offering investors the opportunity to purchase shares well below their NAV. A fund may be trading at a discount due to poor fund performance, improper management skills, or lower distribution levels relative to peers or to market expectations.

Closed-end fund premiums and discounts tend to persist for long periods of time, and often there has to be an external action that triggers a change in the premium or discount.

One such external action would be for the fund to buy back its own shares like Highland Income Fund (HFRO) decided to do in May 2023. A form of closed-end fund arbitrage involves buying a closed-end fund trading at a larger than usual discount to NAV and waiting for that discount to close.

Statistical arbitrage involves tracking the price movements of multiple stocks and finding two or more that usually tend to trade in unison. For example, if PepsiCo's (NASDAQ: PEP) stock were to go up, investors can reasonably expect Coca-Cola's (NYSE: KO) stock to also go up. The stat arb trade kicks in when two securities that were previously trading in close correlation with each other suddenly diverge. The stat arb system would put on a trade with the expectation that these two securities will once again converge in terms of their correlation but not necessarily their price. These systems for identifying and trading stat arb strategies are usually automated using computer programs and are mostly adopted by professional investors.

The Elon Musk–Twitter saga

Our focus in this chapter is the strategy of merger arbitrage, and the acquisition of Twitter by Elon Musk in 2022 provides the perfect backdrop for understanding the strategy.

Twitter (NASDAQ: TWTR) has been called everything from "the digital town square" to "the clown car that fell into a gold mine." I recollect people being surprised a few years ago when I told them Twitter was generating more than $2bn in revenue each year through advertising and selling access to its data. Despite significant ups and downs in the stock price, its revenue has increased in eight of its nine years as a public company, rising from $317m in 2012 to north of $5bn in 2021.

Bottom-line profits were more volatile, and unfortunately shareholders had been left in the back seat of the clown car. Long-term investors, like me, that had held the stock for several years felt that the company had barely scratched the surface in terms of what it could accomplish. A part-time CEO at the helm who was attempting to manage two large publicly traded companies in Twitter and Block (NYSE: SQ) simultaneously did not help.

Elon Musk had an outsized presence on Twitter with a following that far exceeded that of Twitter co-founder Jack Dorsey. Mr. Musk had seen how instrumental Twitter was in building momentum for Tesla and also happened to be friends with Mr. Dorsey.

He quietly started building a stake in Twitter in early 2022. In a regulatory filing with the SEC on April 4, he revealed that he had acquired over 9% of the company.

The short story

The short version of what transpired between Elon Musk and Twitter goes something like along these lines:

EM: I have a stake in Twitter and would like to get involved in some way.

Twitter: Sure, how about joining our board of directors?

[Sidebar conversations with Jack Dorsey.]

[Sidebar conversations with Twitter's CEO Parag Agarwal.]

EM: Forget about joining the board, I want to buy the whole company.

Twitter: We are not for sale.

EM: You have a huge issue with bots that I want to solve.

[The bots issue was well known, detailed in SEC filings, and Twitter had both automated and manual systems to clear out a million bots a day.[3]]

EM: I will go directly to your shareholders if you don't agree to sell.

[Posts a poll on Twitter. There are rumors about several private equity firms getting involved.]

Twitter: We are going to adopt a "poison pill provision."

[A poison pill is a defense mechanism that companies can adopt to stop a hostile acquisition. The mechanism allows them to issue a large number of shares, essentially diluting the stake of the hostile acquirer.]

EM: I've lined up $46.5bn in financing. $54.20 per share is my final offer.

[Gets commitments from a number of existing Twitter investors, including Jack Dorsey, to roll over their stake into the new private company. Also receives commitments from various institutional and ultra-wealthy private investors like Oracle's Larry Ellison.]

Twitter: Alright, we give in. You can have the company.

[Growth stocks continue their big decline and social media companies are hit hard. War breaks out in Ukraine.]

EM: You have a serious bots issue. I am putting the deal on hold.

Twitter: A deal with a merger agreement cannot be put "on hold."

EM: You have not fulfilled your obligations; I am pulling out.

Twitter: We'll see you in court.

[The parties each argue their case in court. They settle outside and close the deal at the agreed-upon price.]

The full story

The complete version of what transpired is as follows:

Mr. Musk had been engaging in conversations about joining Twitter's board of directors but then switched gears and decided to make an offer for the whole company.

Following the $54.20 per share acquisition offer and indications that he had financing lined up, the board of directors engaged with Musk on April 25, 2022, and agreed to a deal.

A merger agreement was inked between the two parties that laid out:

- terms about the final price for Twitter,
- when the deal was expected to close,
- information about any other bidders,
- the kind of regulatory approvals the deal would require,
- approvals from other countries that Twitter does business in,
- termination fees payable if the deal did not go through,
- and a whole lot more.

Such merger agreements can often run to 100 pages or more. In a different time, several decades ago, fund managers that focused on the merger arbitrage strategy would pay someone to get hold of the physical copy of the merger agreement as soon as it was filed with the SEC and rush it to them or call in with the details.

These days you can pull up a copy from EDGAR, within minutes of it being filed with the SEC. Twitter's stock closed at $51.70, or about 5% below the $54.20 acquisition price, shortly after the deal was announced. Regular long-term investors of Twitter might exit after a deal is announced, and investors like me that use the merger arbitrage strategy step in.

Merger arbitrage is also known as risk arbitrage, and as the name implies, arbitrageurs are willing to take the risk that the deal might not close. If *this* deal had not closed, Twitter's stock could have dropped back to levels it was at before the deal was announced or before the unsolicited bid by Mr. Musk. In return for this risk, arbitrageurs expect to capture the difference between the current market price and the price at which the company is expected to be acquired. This difference is referred to as the "spread" on the deal.

The acquisition of Twitter by Elon Musk turned out to have more twists and turns than a spy novel, and the entire saga will eventually be the subject of business school case studies, law school case studies, books, and potentially even a TV series.

By July 11, 2022, the price of Twitter had dropped to $32.65, more than $21 below the price in the merger agreement, and the spread on the deal had widened to a whopping 66%. If an investor purchased shares of Twitter as of the close on that day, they stood to make a return of 66% in less than six months if the deal closed by the end of 2022.

Why was the market discounting the price of Twitter so significantly despite a signed merger agreement? After a whirlwind romance and some initial resistance, Twitter's board of directors and management agreed to sell the company to Elon Musk. Most acquirers go through a lengthy due diligence process before they make a bid for a company, and by the time a merger agreement is inked they have a very good understanding of the business they are acquiring.

The bloom came off the rose for Mr. Musk very rapidly after he signed on the dotted line, and he wanted to get out of the deal. He started challenging Twitter in public about its issues with bots and disparaging its employees, although a specific clause in the merger agreement prohibited him from doing so.

At one point he tweeted that the deal was on hold, sparking speculation that he was attempting to walk away or force Twitter's board to renegotiate the deal.

Why was Mr. Musk suddenly getting cold feet? 2022 turned out to be a challenging year for markets. Growth stocks that had formerly been the darlings of Wall Street were suddenly out of favor and their prices were in free fall. High growth companies that had been spending a lot of money on ads in their quest to find new customers started scaling back their marketing expenses, and social media companies like Meta Platforms, Twitter, Snap, Pinterest and Nextdoor were impacted. The conflict in Ukraine also turned into a full-fledged war, and inflation in the U.S. was near a four-decade high.

Mr. Musk had been selling some of his Tesla stock to fund the purchase of Twitter and it did not help that Tesla was also declining with the market.

There is no concept of putting a "deal on hold" or pulling out of the deal once a definitive merger agreement has been signed. All those tweets by Elon were a ploy to get the board to renegotiate, and the board publicly indicated that they were not willing to play ball.

Definitive merger agreements usually have a "specific performance" clause that outlines how a company can sue its acquirer, either compelling them to complete the merger or holding them liable for damages. A

Image 2.1: Twitter deal timeline

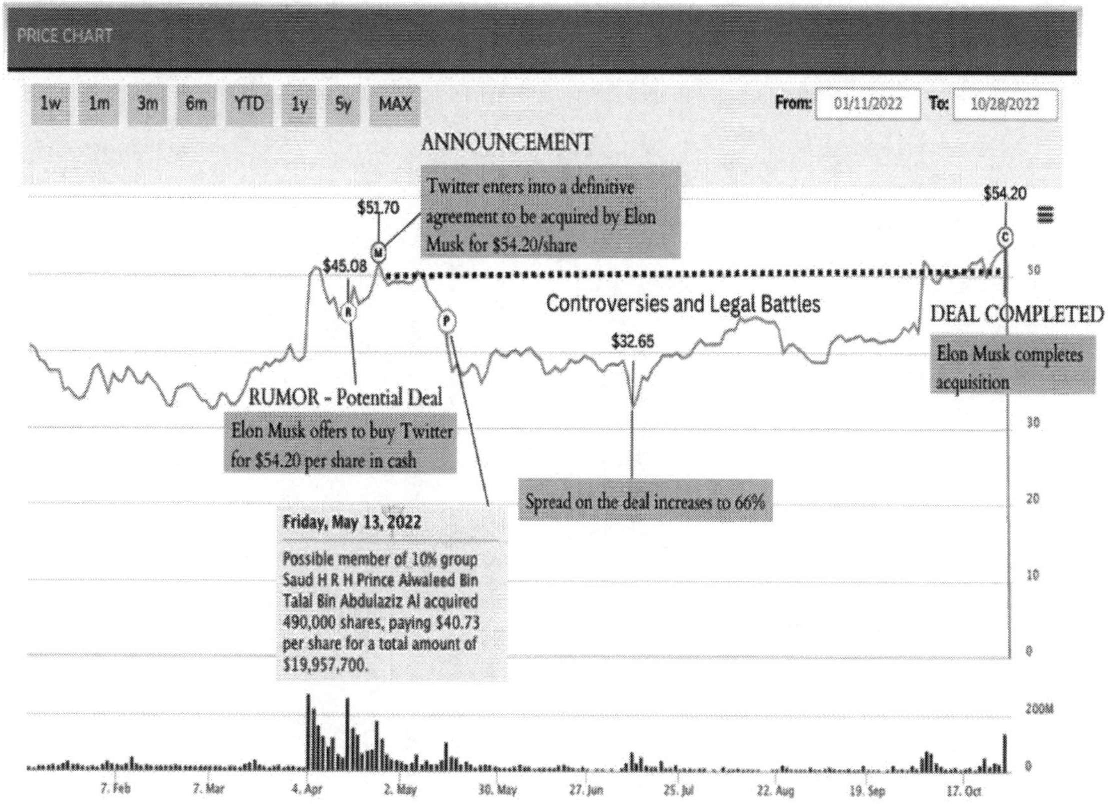

PRICE CHART

| 1w | 1m | 3m | 6m | YTD | 1y | 5y | MAX |

From: 01/11/2022   To: 10/28/2022

ANNOUNCEMENT

Twitter enters into a definitive agreement to be acquired by Elon Musk for $54.20/share

$54.20

$51.70

$45.08

RUMOR – Potential Deal

Elon Musk offers to buy Twitter for $54.20 per share in cash

Friday, May 13, 2022

Possible member of 10% group Saud H R H Prince Alwaleed Bin Talal Bin Abdulaziz Al acquired 490,000 shares, paying $40.73 per share for a total amount of $19,957,700.

Controversies and Legal Battles

$32.65

Spread on the deal increases to 66%

DEAL COMPLETED

Elon Musk completes acquisition

50

30

20

10

0

200M

0

7. Feb   7. Mar   4. Apr   2. May   30. May   27. Jun   25. Jul   22. Aug   19. Sep   17. Oct

Source: InsideArbitrage.com

29

misconception that most investors who were not steeped in the world of mergers and acquisitions had was that Mr. Musk could get out of the deal by paying the termination fee. But it is not easy for an acquirer to just walk away and pay the termination fee, which in Twitter's case was $1bn.

Merger agreements are airtight legal documents that have only a few specific clauses for how someone could get out of the agreement. For an acquiring party to get out of an agreement they must prove that there was a Material Adverse Change (MAC), which in some ways is similar to the *force majeure* clause you often find in contracts. A force majeure clause refers to an "act of God" event like an earthquake or tornado that neither party to the contract could be held accountable for.

Companies can sue their acquirer in court to "make them perform" and close the merger if the acquirer attempts to walk away after the merger agreement is signed. Depending on where the company is incorporated, most of these cases end up in the Delaware Court of Chancery. Such was the case with the dispute between Mr. Musk and Twitter.

Over one million businesses, including 60% of Fortune 500 companies, are incorporated in Delaware because the state does not impose any corporate taxes on companies that are registered in the state but don't do any business in Delaware. The other reason is the state's well respected and established court, the Delaware Court of Chancery, that handles business disputes. The decisions of the court are handed down by judges with expertise in corporate law, rather than being agreed upon by juries.

Unless the acquirer can prove that there was a MAC, the court is likely to make the acquirer perform and close the merger. Usually the parties settle out of court by closing the merger at the agreed-upon terms or at a small discount to the original price.

During the early days of Covid-19, some acquirers did attempt to walk away by claiming the pandemic was a MAC, but were eventually forced to complete their acquisitions, albeit in some cases at a lower price. Forescout Technologies filed a complaint with the Delaware Court of Chancery in

May 2020 asserting that Advent International had violated the terms of their merger agreement. Less than a month later, the two companies agreed to a renegotiated $29 per share acquisition price compared to the original $33 per share all-cash price, and the deal closed in August 2020.

The highest-profile battle during Covid was between LVMH and Tiffany, in which the former, a European luxury company that holds 75 brands including Louis Vuitton, Christian Dior, Dom Perignon, Tag Hauer and Sephora, attempted to walk away from its $16.2bn all-cash acquisition of American jeweler Tiffany. You know how this story ends. In our November 2020 Merger Arbitrage Mondays post titled "Tiffany Rises From The Dead" we outlined how the companies decided to settle their pending litigation in the Delaware Chancery Court and agreed to a price of $131.50 per share compared to the original deal, which was struck at $135 per share in cash.

While Advent managed to finagle a 12.12% discount on its deal for Forescout, LVMH only managed a discount of less than 3%. Sometimes you have to pay up for quality.

In much the same way Tiffany took LVMH to court, Twitter sued Elon Musk in the Delaware Court of Chancery, and Mr. Musk tried to delay the start of the case. Instead of allowing this, chancellor of the court Kathaleen McCormick, the first woman to lead Delaware's 230-year-old court, decided to pick up the case herself.

In an attempt to make his case about Twitter's spam bot issue, Mr. Musk's lawyers tried to bury Twitter in discovery by requesting so much data that it would be a significant burden on Twitter to comply. Delaware's judge threw out this request, stating:

> Defendants' data requests are absurdly broad. Read literally, defendants' documents request would require plaintiff to produce trillions upon trillions of data points reflecting all of the data Twitter might possibly store for each of the approximately 200 million accounts included in its mDAU count every day for

nearly three years. Plaintiff has difficulty quantifying the burden of responding to that request because no one in their right mind has ever tried to undertake such an effort.

The defendant here is Elon Musk, the plaintiff is Twitter, and mDAU stands for monetizable daily active users, a metric that is commonly used by social media companies to track the level of activity on their platforms.

Mr. Musk attempted to avert legal proceedings by indicating that he was willing to close the deal on the original terms. But after months of Mr. Musk's disparaging Twitter and its executives in public, Twitter did not want to take his word and wanted the case to proceed as planned.

In the midst of proceedings, Elon Musk's lawyers mentioned issues brought up by Twitter's former security chief, Peiter "Mudge" Zatko, who had filed a whistleblower complaint about how Twitter had lax security controls and issues with spam.

Anyone who had followed Twitter for any length of time was aware of the operational issues the company faced, how in its early days the site would constantly go down, and the presence of spam bots on the platform. In fact Mr. Musk had publicly stated that he wanted to rid the platform of spam bots, indicating he was aware of the issue.

Elon Musk's lawyers tried to argue that Twitter would have hidden accusations such as those made by Mudge even if Mr. Musk had done in-depth due diligence on the company before signing a definitive merger agreement. The Honorable Kathaleen McCormick's response was one for the record books when she said:

> We don't know what would have happened in diligence because there wasn't any due diligence, right?

After a few days of deliberation, the Twitter case was temporarily put on hold when Mr. Musk indicated he was going to close the transaction. The Honorable Kathaleen McCormick made it clear that she would schedule the lawsuit to resume in November if the deal was not closed by 5pm on October 28.

The deal eventually closed on October 27, at the originally agreed upon price of $54.20 per share.

Spreads, closing dates, and annualized returns

Spreads on deals can be large, such as the case with Microsoft's acquisition of gaming company Activision Blizzard, in which Microsoft (NASDAQ: MSFT) agreed to pay $95 per share in cash for Activision (NASDAQ: ATVI), but it was possible to purchase Activision for $78 on the open market in May 2023. The spread or the return on this investment was nearly 22% at that time as you can see in Image 2.2.

Image 2.2: Activision—Microsoft deal spread

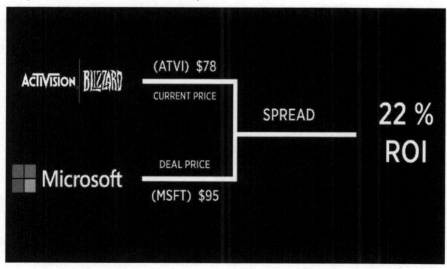

Source: InsideArbitrage

I track the spreads for all active U.S. deals on my website InsideArbitrage in a program called the Merger Arbitrage Tool (MAT).

Image 2.3: Merger arbitrage tool

Acquirer	Target	Deal Type	Closing Value	Deal Price	Est. Close Date	Return
Unity (U)	IS	Stock	$3.61 B	$6.37	12/31/22	58.79%
Shift Technologies, Inc. (SFT)	LOTZ	Stock	$1.23 M	$0.85	12/31/22	41.89%
JetBlue Airways Corporation (JBLU)	SAVE	Cash + Stock	$7.6 B	$33.50	6/30/24	36.35%
MaxLiner, Inc. (MXL)	SIMO	Special*	$8 B	$109.62	6/30/23	32.69%
Intercontinental Exchange, Inc. (ICE)	BKI	Cash	$16 B	$85.00	6/30/23	26.60%

Source: InsideArbitrage

The spread on the Activision Blizzard deal is large because there is a chance that the Federal Trade Commission (FTC) in the United States, or other foreign regulators, might attempt to block it for anti-competitive reasons. Sony (NYSE: SONY) and Electronic Arts (NASDAQ: EA) are probably not too thrilled with the prospect of Microsoft owning Activision's popular gaming franchises like Call of Duty, Starcraft, World of Warcraft, Diablo, etc.

Gamers sometimes purchase gaming consoles based on which titles are exclusively available on those consoles. The popular first-person shooter game Halo is only available on the Xbox console and Windows PCs. Locking down both Halo and Call of Duty on a single platform like Xbox could give Microsoft an advantage over Sony's PlayStation.

There are other deals with small spreads such as Oracle's acquisition of electronic health records software company Cerner, which traded at a tiny spread of just 1.3% as of this writing. Why would arbitrageurs want to get involved in a deal that provides a small return of 1.3%? They assess the probability of the Cerner deal closing as very high and don't mind picking up 1.3% in a low-yield environment. In fact, looking at over a decade of deals from the InsideArbitrage database, I have observed that around 95%

of all deals with a definitive merger agreement end up consummating their merger successfully.

Since deals tend to close relatively quickly (most of them within four months), arbitrageurs can reinvest the money that frees up after a deal closes and improve their annual returns.

Acquisition targets that have been paying a dividend often continue to pay the dividend until the acquisition closes. This can provide a nice little bonus and enhance the return for a deal. If a target company has a 4% annual yield (a generous dividend as of this writing) and the deal is expected to close in six months, picking up dividends during those six months can enhance returns by 2%. Obviously not all acquirers are so generous and will sometimes specify in the merger agreement that the target will stop paying dividends at a certain time.

If an arbitrageur made a 4.5% return on Alphabet's (NASDAQ: GOOG) acquisition of Mandiant (MNDT) in four months and can repeat the process three times in a year with deals sporting similar spreads, they can make 13.5% in a year without taking compounding into account. This is one of the reasons arbitrageurs are often focused on the "annualized returns" of each deal. For a deal that closes in one quarter and that sports a spread of 4%, the annualized returns are a very attractive 16%.

When you start thinking of merger arbitrage opportunities in terms of their annualized returns, the expected closing date becomes very important. Companies cannot provide a specific closing date because there are several unknowns when the deal is announced.

- Will shareholders approve the deal, or will enough shareholders tender their shares?

- If the deal requires regulatory approval, will it go through without any issues?

- Will the financing for the deal take longer than expected?

Companies often indicate that the deal will close in, for example, the fourth quarter of the year, the second half of next year, mid-2024 or the third fiscal quarter of 2023. To calculate the annualized returns, I use a conservative approach when it comes to the closing date. For a deal announced in 2023, if a company indicates that they will close the deal in the second half of next year, I use December 31, 2024 as the closing date.

Starting from this conservative closing date as a baseline, you can then make adjustments depending on how long deals are taking on average to close, looking at sector-specific closing times, analyzing the regulatory or financing risks the deal faces, etc. For example, pharmaceutical deals where a large company like Pfizer is acquiring a smaller drug company often tend to close in as little as three months. On the other hand, semiconductor deals tend to take much longer because of national security concerns and approvals needed from multiple countries. Banking and insurance deals also take longer as numerous regulators are involved in the approval process.

Analyzing a list of 2,320 completed deals between 2010 and 2022, I noticed that on average deals took 131 days to close. The median time to completion was just 107 days, implying that some outlier deals like the acquisition of Change Healthcare by UnitedHealth Group (UNH) that took 635 days to complete or the acquisition of Xilinx by AMD that took 475 days to complete, skew the average.

As we mentioned earlier, most deals close in four months, however the impact of deal delays can be significant on an arbitrageur. If you were expecting a deal with a 4% spread to close in four months, generating a very respectable 12% annualized returns, a delay in the deal that makes it close in six months would change your annualized returns to just 8%.

Another issue to keep in mind is that companies include an "outside date" in their definitive merger agreements. This date is usually well after the expected closing date and most deals close long before this outside date. However, if for some reason the deal gets delayed significantly and reaches the outside date, the parties can either terminate the deal or extend the outside date. They also have the option to extend the outside date multiple times.

Every once in a while, a deal will trade at a negative spread. As in, investors are willing to pay more than the deal price to buy stock. We saw this happen when the home builder D. R. Horton (NYSE: DHI) announced a deal for Vidler Water Resources for $15.75 per share in cash. Vidler Water Resources holds water rights in several western states, and with the western U.S. in a severe drought, water rights can be worth a lot. This is one of the reasons Vidler Water Resources traded as high as $17.24 (or a negative spread of 9.5%) right after the deal was announced. Existing investors and new investors that purchased after the deal was announced were hoping that a third party might emerge to buy the company, creating a bidding war between D. R. Horton and that third party for Vidler. The deal eventually closed at the agreed-upon price of $15.75, and arbitrageurs that were willing to pay a premium in the hopes of a higher offer were disappointed.

It is not uncommon to see competing offers for deals, and the pace of competing offers has increased in recent years given easy access to cheap capital. Sometimes this triggers a bidding war that lasts several rounds, much to the delight of arbitrageurs. We saw a bidding war between JetBlue (NASDAQ: JBLU) and Frontier Airline (NASDAQ: ULCC) related to the acquisition of Spirit Airlines (NYSE: SAVE) that lasted four months. After seven rounds of back and forth between the companies, JetBlue won the bidding war by offering a price that was 32% more than Frontier's offer and with a larger termination fee of $400m that JetBlue would pay Spirit in case regulators blocked the deal.

Another bidding war that erupted was the battle between AT&T (NYSE: T) and Verizon (NYSE: VZ) for Straight Path Communications. This saw the stock price nearly double from the original deal price. Critics of the merger arbitrage strategy often focus on deal failures and forget the upside provided by deals that end up in bidding wars.

Next we turn to the different types of deals (all-cash deals, cash-plus-stock deals, etc.), the various stages of a deal, and different ways to use the merger arbitrage strategy.

Deal types, CVRs and methods to capture the spread

In this section we dive into various types of deals, and how arbitrageurs can capture the spread in each of these situations.

As of the morning of April 26, 2022, Twitter's stock was trading at $50 per share with a spread of around 8%. If an arbitrageur bought Twitter on that day and the deal closed by the end of the year, they could have made a return of 8% in a little over eight months—an annualized return of 12%. The investor would have cash in their account when the deal closed because this was an "all cash" deal, just like Microsoft's acquisition of Activision Blizzard (ATVI).

Not all deals are paid in cash. There are other flavors of deals including:

- All-stock deals,
- Cash-plus-stock deals,
- Cash-or-stock deals,
- Deals that include a collar mechanism,
- Special conditions and CVRs

All-stock deals

The acquisition of Metromile by the insurance company Lemonade (LMND) was an all-stock deal. Shareholders of Metromile received one share of Lemonade for every 19 shares of Metromile they held. The spread on the deal was 14.06% on May 6, 2022. If the deal had closed as expected by the end of June 2022, the annualized return would have worked out to 93.31%. The deal closing was delayed and it eventually closed about a month later on July 28, 2022.

One challenge with capturing the spread in an all-stock deal is that any movement in the price of the acquiring company will also impact the price of the target company like Metromile. For example, let us assume you purchased Metromile for $1 per share on May 6, 2022 and the deal value was $1.14 per share, providing you with a 14% profit on the arbitrage situation. Let us assume that on the next day, Lemonade unexpectedly announced some bad news and the stock price dropped sharply by 20%. Since the Metromile deal is an all-stock deal, you can reasonably expect that the stock of Metromile would have also dropped by approximately 20%. Instead of capturing a 14% profit on the deal when it closed, you are now sitting on a loss in the position and have no idea how much money you will receive when the deal finally closes. To avoid a situation like this, arbitrageurs "lock in the spread" on all stock deals by selling short the stock of the acquiring company.

Short sellers initially sell shares they don't have by borrowing them from a broker and eventually plan to buy them back at a lower price to return the borrowed stock to the broker. In other words, they sell high and buy low if all goes according to plan. If on the other hand, the price of the stock rises, the short sellers end up with a loss and at some point are forced to cover their position by buying back the stock and closing their short position. Shorting in arbitrage is not done to profit from a drop in the stock price of the company being shorted but to lock in the spread on the deal.

To capture the spread on the Metromile deal, an arbitrageur would have sold one share of Lemonade short for every 19 shares of Metromile they owned.

When the deal closed, the Lemonade shares they received canceled out the short position and generated a return of around 14%. This did not take into account any borrowing fees on the short position.

It also did not take into account the dividends an arbitrageur has to pay on the short position. When you own a stock, you collect any regular or special dividends paid by the company. In contrast, if you borrow the stock of the acquiring company and sell it short, you are now responsible for paying any dividends the acquirer might issue to the person you borrowed the stock from.

The risk with all-stock deals is that if the deal fails, not only is Metromile likely to drop to pre-deal prices, Lemonade stock is likely to go up as arbitrageurs cover their short positions or the market is generally happy with Lemonade getting out of the deal. This delivers a double whammy to the arbitrageur in case of a failed deal.

The challenges with shorting is one of the reasons many arbitrageurs prefer to stick to all-cash deals.

Cash-plus-stock deals

Another common deal type is one where the acquirer pays for part of the deal in cash and part of it in stock. A good example of this kind of deal was the $2.5bn acquisition of Cooper Tire by Goodyear Tire & Rubber (GT). Under the terms of the transaction, Cooper Tire shareholders received $41.75 per share in cash and a little less than one share of Goodyear (0.907 share to be precise) per Cooper share.

The spread on this deal wasn't particularly large but at two points after the deal was announced, the spread was a little over 3%. To lock in the spread on this deal, Cooper shareholders would have had to short nine shares of Goodyear for every 10 shares they held. When the deal closed in June 2021, just 105 days after it was announced, Cooper shareholders received $41.75 in cash and the Goodyear shares they received canceled out the short position.

Cash-or-stock deals

A fourth kind of deal is the cash-*or*-stock kind, in which shareholders must elect to receive either cash or shares of the acquiring company. These kinds of deals usually have a proration clause where, for example, 70% of the consideration is paid in shares and the rest in cash. Shareholders make their election for cash or stock and then the company prorates if too many shareholders are asking for cash and not enough elected to receive shares. Capturing the spread in these situations is tricky, as you might not know if you will be paid in cash, stock, or some combination of the two.

Collar mechanisms

A fifth type of deal is one where a "collar mechanism" is introduced. Instead of the stock portion of the deal being a fixed ratio (such as 0.907 share of Goodyear for each Cooper share), it can vary depending on what happens to the price of the acquiring company's stock. A good example of this is Take-Two Interactive's (TTWO) acquisition of Zynga that was announced in January 2022 and was consummated a little over four months later. Zynga stockholders were supposed to receive $3.50 in cash and $6.361 in shares of Take-Two for each share of Zynga. However, this $6.361 portion was subject to a "collar."

As defined in the merger agreement:

> If Take-Two's 20-day volume weighted average price ("VWAP") ending on the third trading day prior to closing is in a range from $156.50 to $181.88, the exchange ratio would be adjusted to deliver total consideration value of $9.86 per Zynga share (including $6.36 of equity value and $3.50 in cash). If the VWAP exceeds the higher end of that range, the exchange ratio would be 0.0350 per share, and if the VWAP falls below the lower end of that range, the exchange ratio would be 0.0406.

If that makes your head spin, you are not alone. In simpler terms, Take-Two had structured the deal in such a way that a little over 64% of the deal value paid to Zynga shareholders would be in Take-Two stock. The condition in the merger agreement stipulated that depending on where Take-Two's stock price ends up a few days before the deal closes, the amount of Take-Two stock Zynga shareholders would receive can go up or down.

The deal finally closed on May 23, 2022 and Take-Two indicated that Zynga shareholders received $3.50 in cash and 0.0406 shares of Take-Two. When the deal was announced in January 2022, Take-Two's stock was trading above $210 per share. By the time the deal closed, Take-Two's stock had dropped sharply to $123.62. The ratio used for the stock portion of the deal was at the low end of the collar specified in the merger agreement and hence Zynga shareholders received 0.0406 shares of Take-Two per share of Zynga. This is one of the reasons I classify these kinds of deals "special conditions" deals in our Merger Arbitrage Tool, and the spread on these kinds of deals has to be constantly recalculated.

Special conditions and CVRs

There are unique situations that might affect the spread, such as special dividends paid around the close of a deal. We have seen this happen with UnitedHealth Group's (NYSE: UNH) acquisition of Change Healthcare. After running into regulatory issues, UnitedHealth decided to sweeten the $25.75 per share all-cash original deal by adding a $2 per share special dividend that would be paid out at or near the closing.

Two other unique situations include: a portion of the target company spun out as a separate public company right before the merger closes, like we had with Blackstone's acquisition of Bluerock Residential Growth REIT (BRG), and a portion of the merger consideration paid out as Contingent Value Rights or CVRs.

CVRs are often called earn-outs in private markets, and Joel Greenblatt referred to them as merger securities in his book *You Can Be a Stock Market Genius*.[4] I find CVRs fascinating as they include a kicker, where investors get one or more additional payments in the future if certain milestones are met after the closing of the deal. If the deal is trading at a positive spread and risks to closing are low, you can think of the CVR as a free or nearly free lottery ticket.

These kinds of CVRs are often seen in pharma/biotech types of deals where the company being acquired has drugs in their pipeline that could get approved long after the deal has closed. I have also seen CVRs attached to the disposal of real estate in deals such as the acquisition of Safeway by Cerberus Capital Management. Not all CVRs pay out, but for the ones that do, like the acquisition of Safeway in 2015 or the acquisition of Tobira Therapeutics by Allergan in 2016, they provide a sweet additional payout. I participated in both those deals because the merger spreads were sufficient to make the CVR almost free.

Next steps and regulatory processes

The earlier sections of this chapter were related to the mechanics of the merger arbitrage strategy. We will now explore the next steps in the merger process and especially the regulatory element, which has a huge impact on the probability of the deal closing and hence the spread available to arbitrageurs.

Shopping around

Certain merger agreements have a "go shop" period where the target company can go out to solicit additional interest. This usually gives them 25 to 45 days to drum up a competing bid.

Since most deals are already shopped by investment banks before the merger agreement is signed, we rarely see a new bid emerge during the go shop period. For example, the go shop period for Berkshire Hathaway's (BRK.A) acquisition of Alleghany (Y) did not yield a new bid.

Shareholder resistance

Most deals also require shareholder approval and corporate governance firms like Institutional Shareholder Services (ISS) usually weigh in with their recommendation. It is not common to see shareholders attempt to block the deal, but it does happen from time to time. One example was WindAcre Partners objecting to the acquisition of Nielsen Holding by Brookfield and activist investment firm Elliott Investment Management in April 2022. To combat the deal, WindAcre started buying more shares and eventually built a 27% stake in Nielsen. The deal was allowed to close after Nielsen struck a deal with WindAcre and certain other investors that allowed WindAcre to invest an additional $500m into Nielsen after the deal closed. The deal finally closed in October 2022, 196 days after it was announced.

T. Rowe Price objected to Oracle's (NYSE: ORCL) acquisition of Netsuite in 2016, saying the purchase price was too low, but was unable to stop the deal. The fact that Oracle founder Larry Ellison already owned 40% of NetSuite did not help T. Rowe Price. Rite Aid (NYSE: RAD) shareholders were not too keen on the company merging with Albertsons and killed that deal in 2018. So did the shareholders of Five9 (NASDAQ: FIVN) in 2021 when they rejected an all-stock deal with Zoom (NASDAQ: ZM). Considering how things played out for tech stocks since September 2021, Five9 shareholders would have been better off taking the deal. Rite Aid dropped into penny stock territory in August 2023 and the company is expected to file for bankruptcy as of this writing, a fate that could have been avoided had its shareholders not voted against the Albertsons deal.

Regulatory considerations

Moving on to the regulatory process, companies that are involved in a large merger or acquisition are required, under the Hart-Scott-Rodino (HSR) Act, to file a pre-merger notification and wait for government review. This is known as an HSR filing and starts a 30-day clock for the government. The threshold for an HSR filing is $111.4m in 2023 and is adjusted each year. Companies are required to file with both the FTC and the Department of Justice (DOJ). Only one of these governmental agencies will review the deal to determine whether there are anti-competitive concerns and if allowing the deal to proceed would give the combined company unfair pricing power or access to large troves of data.

There are several ways things can play out once the 30-day clock starts:

- The FTC or the DOJ may grant early termination of the HSR waiting period if they don't need to do a deep review of the deal and the companies can proceed with consummating it.

- The 30-day clock on the HSR filing may run out with no action from either the FTC or DOJ.

- The companies, after discussions with the FTC or DOJ, may voluntarily pull their HSR filing and refile to reset the clock and give the agencies more time to review the deal.

- The FTC or the DOJ, after completing their initial review, might seek additional information and documents from the companies. This is known as the "second request," and the companies cannot consummate the merger until they provide all the information requested.

- The FTC or the DOJ might sue to block the deal if they deem the deal to be anti-competitive. Staples was blocked from acquiring Office Depot when a judge sided with the FTC. More recently, the DOJ sued to block UnitedHealth Group (NYSE: UNH) from acquiring Change Healthcare (NASDAQ: CHNG) on February 23, 2022.

The two companies decided to take their chances in court instead of walking away from the deal. Much to the delight of arbitrageurs, they won the case on September 19, 2022, and the deal closed two weeks later.

Beyond the FTC and DOJ, other regulators may have to approve the deal depending on the industry and countries involved. For example, insurance company deals and mergers of utilities are likely to take a long time as multiple state agencies have to provide their approvals if these companies operate in more than one state.

Cross-border or international deals go through a review process by an agency called the Committee on Foreign Investment in the United States (CFIUS). If CFIUS deems the deal to be against the national interests of the United States, they can stop it, as was the case with the acquisition of South Korean semiconductor company Magnachip (NYSE: MX) by a Chinese private equity firm. In this case CFIUS decided to investigate a foreign domiciled company because it identified risks to the national security of the United States arising from the acquisition. CFIUS also recommended blocking the acquisition of Portland, Oregon-based semiconductor firm Lattice Semiconductor (NASDAQ: LSCC) by a Chinese venture capital firm in 2017. A pattern of issues with semiconductor deals has started to emerge, and semiconductor deals often tend to trade at large spreads.

Regulators in other countries have also blocked deals. China's State Administration for Market Regulation (SAMR), which is China's equivalent of the U.S. FTC, ran out the clock on Qualcomm's acquisition of NXP Semiconductors (NASDAQ: NXPI) by not making a decision until the merger hit its "outside date" (the deadline by which the companies had to complete the merger).

The UK's Competition and Markets Authority (CMA) was concerned about the impact on competition if Illumina (NASDAQ: ILMN) was allowed to complete its acquisition of Pacific Biosciences of California

(NASDAQ: PACB). It was ultimately the FTC that killed that deal in late 2019. In other words, even if the deal is not a cross-border deal, countries in which the company has operations also have to approve it. The Twitter deal required approval from Japan, the UK, and the European Commission but thankfully not China because Twitter was banned in China.

In the final section about merger arbitrage we cover various ways to express the merger arbitrage strategy by buying stock, using options, and more.

Different ways to express a merger arbitrage strategy

The simplest way to implement a merger arbitrage strategy would be through a deal that goes through a shareholder vote, like the all-cash deal for Twitter. You would buy shares of Twitter, wait for the deal to close, and get $54.20 for each share you sold, in cash, in your account once the deal closes.

If the deal is structured as a tender offer, you would have to call your broker and tender the shares. We discuss tender offers in more detail in our chapter on stock buybacks. If you forget to tender your shares and the buyer ends up getting a majority of shares, they will complete what is known as a "second step" merger and squeeze out the remaining shareholders by giving them cash.

The rules that define what a majority is depend on the state in which the company is incorporated. Be aware that in some countries, there may not be an automatic "second step" merger, and you have to call in to tender your shares.

For international mergers there may be other rules to be aware of including the completion of certain tax-related forms. For example, Israel requires you to complete a form to avoid withholding taxes on the money paid when the deal completes. Your broker can usually help you find any relevant forms and, once completed, you also send the forms to your broker unless the company has identified a third-party firm to handle this process.

Once you get past the simple cases, there can be quite a bit of creativity involved in how arbitrageurs express the strategy, especially when combined with stock options.

For investors that are not familiar with stock options, I have provided a brief introduction below and then discuss four different ways options can be used in merger arbitrage. If you have already used options or understand them, you can skip ahead to the "Options in arbitrage" section of this chapter.

A brief introduction to options

Stock options provide investors the privilege of buying or selling a certain stock at a specified price for a period of time. The stock is referred to as the "underlying instrument," the price is referred to as the "strike price" and the end of that period of time is referred to as the "expiration date."

An option that gives you the privilege to buy a stock at a certain price is called a call option. An option that gives you the privilege to sell a stock at a certain price is called a put option. The option gives you this privilege for a period that can range from a few days to a few years.

Let us start with put options, because in many ways they mirror something most of us already use on a daily basis. You can think of put options like an insurance policy. You purchase a car insurance policy, and it protects you from suddenly being on the hook for a large financial liability when an accident occurs. You pay a premium for this policy, and it usually covers you for a specified period of time, which can be extended by paying additional premiums. The premium you pay is a small amount of money compared to the potential liability you might incur from an accident that could cause damage to the car, to its occupants and other parties involved in the accident.

To draw parallels between this car insurance policy and put options let us consider a situation where you have a large amount of Apple stock in your portfolio purchased years ago during the depths of the Covid-19 pandemic at a split-adjusted price of $70 per share. The stock in September 2023 trades a little above $174 per share, leaving you with a large gain on one of your largest stock positions.

It is a beautiful fall day in September 2023, and you are in the market to buy your first home, but current interest rates, which are at multi-decade highs, have given you pause. You don't mind waiting a couple of years to make the purchase but are concerned that the Apple stock you plan to sell to fund your 20% downpayment on the new home might decline over the next two years. Selling now means you have to pay a lot of taxes on the capital gains this year. You might also miss out on any upside from the stock in case Apple releases an Apple car or their latest watch can beam you up to Mars.

On the flipside you are also concerned that Apple's decision to move some of its manufacturing from China to countries like India and Vietnam risks angering Chinese government authorities. China is a very large and important market for Apple products. Recent speculation that the Chinese government plans to ban iPhone use by state-backed companies and government agencies has you spooked.[5] To top it all, the market is trading at an all-time high, increasing your anxiety.

Can you have your cake and eat it too? Financial markets are happy to cater to your wishes as long as you pay them a small premium for the privilege. By purchasing $170 put options on Apple stock expiring in December 2025 for $19 per contract, you can achieve your goals of downside protection, while benefiting from any upside in case Apple stock continues going up.

Let us break down that last sentence to understand what you purchased. It means that until the third Friday of December 2025, you have the ability to sell your Apple stock for $170 even if for some reason it loses half its value and drops from the current $174 per share to just $87 per share by the time December 2025 rolls around.

This little insurance policy costs you $19 per share. Each options contract represents 100 shares and so your total premium for this insurance was $1,900 per 100 shares. If you hold 500 shares in your account, you can buy 5 put option contracts to cover those 500 shares but it will cost you $9,500 in premium. Since these are American-style options, they can be exercised at any time until the date of expiration. If you end up finding the house of your dreams in April 2025 and the price of Apple at that time is $110 per share, you can exercise the put options you purchased and sell those shares for $170 per share. In contrast, European-style options can only be exercised on expiration.

Who is on the other side of that trade you just made by purchasing $170 put options on Apple expiring in December 2025? It is another trader, investor, fund or investment bank that is acting like an insurance company. They want to collect the premium you are willing to pay because they think the probability of Apple dropping below $151 before expiration is low. Since you paid $19 per share up front, their breakeven price on the trade is $151 and not $170. If the stock drops below $151, they make a loss and if the stock trades above that level, they make a profit. Their ideal scenario would be for the stock to trade above $170 at expiration because then the insurance did not have to be used. Let us say the stock is trading at $200 when the put option expires, you will choose to sell on the open market for $200 instead of using the option to sell at $170. The put option then expires, worthless. This would be like someone buying car insurance year after year and paying premiums to the insurance company without ever getting into an accident.

Call options are the opposite of put options in the sense that they give the option buyer the privilege of buying a stock at a specific price (the strike price) until a certain period of time (the expiration date). For example, you are convinced that Apple is going to release a car next year and think that they will capture half of the market for new electric cars in a few years. Each Apple share currently trades at $174 per share. Buying 100 shares would cost you $17,400. You don't have that much money lying around but you do have $4,000 and instead of buying 23 shares of Apple (22.9885 shares to be precise), you want to make a larger bet on 100 shares instead.

While you are convinced Apple will release a new car and both its revenue and earnings will go up sharply, you are not sure about the timing. To give yourself some extra time to let your thesis play out, you pick $170 call options on Apple expiring in December 2025. The premium for these options is $38 per contract, almost double the premium of the put options for the same $170 strike price. The total cost for the trade is $3,800 because each contract represents 100 shares.

There are two reasons the premium on the call option is almost double that of the put options. This call option is what is called "in-the-money" because the strike price is a little below the current price of $174. This means you can exercise the options right after buying them and buy Apple stock for $170, turning a quick $4 per share profit. Although considering the large premium you paid, this does not make any sense. The premium is mostly because of the amount of time the options provide you to buy the stock for $170. The second reason the call options are more expensive is because the market thinks the probability of Apple going up in price by December 2025 is much higher than Apple dropping a lot by that date. The person on the other side of your trade, the writer of this call option, wants to be paid more money to take on this trade.

The person on the other side of both these trades is called an option writer. Think of them like the house in a casino. The house usually has the advantage in most games of chance. They know that while a gambler might occasionally win at a spin of the roulette wheel, over multiple turns of the wheel, the house has an advantage over the gamblers. A majority of options expire worthless, and the option writers often continue collecting premiums from the buyers of options. This happens until a sudden unexpected move in a stock requires them to take a loss, much like the house in the casino when a gambler wins, or an insurance company would in case of an accident.

When an option writer already owns a position in the underlying stock and then sells you call options on that stock, it is called a covered call. If for example Apple's stock jumps to $300 per share by December 2025 because the company launched a car and the next iteration of the iPhone sells like hot cakes, you can now exercise the $170 call options you purchased and buy the stock for $170. You turned a very tidy profit of $92 per share on the trade even after including the $38 per share premium you paid for the options. The person who wrote the covered call now has to sell you their Apple stock at $170 and their total sales price works out to $208 per share after including the premium collected.

Options in arbitrage

To squeeze out extra returns in an arbitrage situation, you can sell covered call options on the existing position and pick up the premium on that option. The call option would ideally expire after the expected closing of the deal. Writing a covered call option would imply that you do not expect a competing bid or higher offer and are willing to give up any additional upside from a potential bidding war. For deals with small spreads where perceived risks are small and the deal is expected to close, the premium on the covered calls may be tiny.

For a cash and stock deal, assuming the shareholder shorted an equivalent number of shares of the acquirer, part of the proceeds will be in cash and the other part in the acquirer's stock, which can close out the short position. If the spread on the deal is large and perceived risk is high, an investor could also purchase put options to protect their downside in case the deal fails.

I was able to do this with Microsoft's 2016 acquisition of LinkedIn, which offered a good spread even after protecting the downside through put options. How far "out of the money" the put options need to be is determined by how much risk you want to take, and the expiration date will depend on when the deal is expected to close. The premium paid for the put options reduces the spread that can be captured, and there is a possibility that the deal will be delayed and the put options expire worthless.

Another way to capture the spread while limiting the downside is by buying call options that expire shortly after the expected close date. I did this with the acquisition of Apollo (the for-profit education company) by the private equity firm Apollo Global Management (NYSE: APO). Once again, you would end up giving up some of the spread to pay for the call option premiums, but the bet could be leveraged because of the inherent leverage afforded by options. The risk with buying naked call options is that if the deal does not close or gets delayed, the option premium is lost.

Investors could also opt to sell put options with strike prices just below the deal price with an expiration date beyond the expected closing date. If the deal closes, you pick up the premium from those options. However, if the deal fails or is delayed, you would be on the hook for buying shares at the strike price. Option premiums for these situations have been very thin in recent years.

Some of these strategies will only work for certain deal types, and each has its own risks and rewards. Once again, there is a reason merger arbitrage is also called risk arbitrage.

Busted deals and other opportunities

Failure in merger arbitrage hurts. When a deal with 5% upside blows up, it can wipe out anywhere from 30% to 50% of your capital. This might be the reason arbitrageurs have gone on to have very successful investing careers after leaving the arbitrage world. They constantly assess the probability of success, try to figure out what could go wrong, and pay attention to details that other investors might ignore.

Investors that trade based on trends or technical indicators look for certain signals or patterns to infer how the future might unfold. Similarly, arbitrageurs can benefit from watching the trend of a spread to determine if a deal is likely to succeed or fail.

In the paper "Characteristics of Risk and Return in Risk Arbitrage" by Mark Mitchell and Todd Pulvino, they discuss how deal spreads for failed mergers tend to be large right after a deal is announced and increase in the days before the deal fails.[6]

Mark Mitchell and Todd Pulvino are co-founders of the investment firm AQR Arbitrage. Prior to founding the firm, Dr. Mitchell was a finance professor at University of Chicago's Booth School of Business and before that at Harvard Business School. Dr. Pulvino was a tenured associate professor of finance at Northwestern University's Kellogg School of Management.

As discussed earlier in this chapter, 95% of all announced deals tend to close and the failure rate was 5% in the data I extracted from the InsideArbitrage database from 2010 to 2022. The summary table in Image 2.4 shows how many deals were consummated, how many failed, deals that received new offers, and those that were active when this was generated at the end of 2022. Since a large number of deals announced in 2022 were still active when this data was analyzed, you can discount the 2022 data but that does not impact the overall results.

Image 2.4: Deal success, failure and new offers by year (2010 to 2022)

Announced Year	Active	Completed	Failed	New Offer	Total	Success Rate
2010		210	10	3	223	94%
2011		193	8		201	96%
2012		201	5		206	98%
2013		182	8	1	191	95%
2014		181	5		186	97%
2015		210	14	6	230	91%
2016		219	6	3	228	96%
2017		200	12	5	217	92%
2018		200	8	1	209	96%
2019		183	5	5	193	95%
2020	1	137	12	4	154	90%
2021	3	204	8	6	221	94%
2022	102	85	2	2	191	98%
Total	**106**	**2,405**	**103**	**36**	**2,650**	**95%**

Source: InsideArbitrage.com database

Now that we have looked at how successful deals and failed deals behave, from the point the deal is announced to the moment it either closes or is terminated, as well as the overall rate of success or failure, let's examine the impact of macroeconomic factors on deals from a dataset that precedes the period covered in the table from Image 2.4.

In the paper "Macroeconomic Drivers Behind Risk Arbitrage Strategy" by OFI Asset Management's Fabienne Cretin, Slimane Bouacha, and Stéphane Dieudonné, the authors analyze 1,911 M&A U.S. and Canadian deals announced between January 1998 and September 2010.[7]

A chart in the paper grabbed my attention as it shows how spreads widen and termination rates go up during bear markets like the ones we experienced in 2001–2003 and 2008–2009. While the average odds of success are around 95%, and there is a very high probability that most announced deals will close, you know what they say about averages: a six-foot-tall person can drown in a river that is on average about five feet deep. In the next section of this chapter, I am going to focus on two case studies of deals that failed because studying failure could help us improve our odds of success. The other reason it is important to pay attention to failed deals is because of the opportunity they offer post-failure.

Considering 95% of deals with a definitive merger agreement close, I have decided to focus on failed deals for the case studies for this chapter because of their disproportionate impact on overall returns for someone using the merger arbitrage strategy.

Case study 1: Rite Aid

Italian billionaire Stefano Pessina started his business empire by taking over his family's pharmaceutical wholesaler business in 1977. Through a series of mergers and acquisitions, the dealmaker known as the "Silver Fox" ended up the CEO and executive chairman of one of the world's largest drugstore chains, Walgreens Boots Alliance (NASDAQ: WBA). The chain operates the Walgreens and Duane Read chains in the U.S., the Boots chain in the U.K., and Benavides in Mexico. It operates a whopping 8,886 drugstores in the U.S. and nearly 4,000 drugstores in five other countries.

In October 2015, Walgreens Boots Alliance struck a deal to acquire the third largest drugstore chain in the U.S., Rite Aid (NYSE: RAD) in a massive $17.2bn deal for $9 per share in cash. At the time of announcement, Rite Aid had 4,600 stores in 31 U.S. states and the District of Columbia.

At the time of the announcement, CVS, Walgreens and Rite Aid were the three largest independent drugstore chains in the U.S., handling about a third of all prescription revenue in the country. The rest was handled by mail order and specialty pharmacies, as well as pharmacies built inside stores like Walmart, Target, Costco, Kroger and Albertsons.

Unfortunately for Walgreens and Rite Aid, just months after the deal was announced Target decided to sell its retail pharmacy business to CVS for $1.9bn, and CVS started managing Target's 1,672 pharmacies, further increasing the proportion of U.S. drug stores owned by the top three chains.

Regulators took a very close look at the deal, and after 21 tumultuous months the two companies called it off. To appease the FTC, the companies entered into an agreement with another drugstore chain, Fred's, to divest 865 Rite Aid stores. That did not satisfy the FTC. More than 15 months after the deal was announced, the two sides recut the deal at a price of $6.50–$7 per share (depending on how many stores Rite Aid would have to divest to satisfy regulators).

Walgreens and Rite Aid eventually were ready to divest as much as 1,200 stores, and Fred's started preparing for this acquisition by adding more directors to its board. Regulators were unwilling to accept this new deal despite the fact that Rite Aid was divesting nearly a quarter of its stores. They pointed to the merger of the grocery chains Albertsons and Safeway in 2015, which was only approved after the companies agreed to divest 168 stores to various companies, with 146 of those stores acquired by Haggen Holdings. Less than a year later, Haggen Holdings ended up filing for chapter 11 bankruptcy and sued Albertsons, which was at that time a private company under private equity ownership.

The FTC had seen this movie before when the car rental giant Hertz acquired rival Dollar Thrifty in 2012. To appease regulators, they sold a certain business segment and 29 rental locations to a company called Franchise Services of North America (FSNA). You guessed it: less than a year later, FSNA filed for bankruptcy. These kinds of bankruptcies of Haggen Holdings and FSNA reduce competition further by making the larger players stronger and is the exact opposite of what the FTC wants.

On June 29, 2017, Walgreens and Rite Aid decided to mutually terminate the deal because of regulatory issues, and Walgreens paid Rite Aid a termination fee of $325m. The story did not end there, and Walgreens under Mr. Pessina's guidance, ended up eventually acquiring 2,186 stores from Rite Aid for $5.175bn.

The slimmed-down Rite Aid was grossly mismanaged in the years following the deal's failure, posting a string of losses. Its stock went on to lose more than 90% of its value. There were a couple of chances of redemption along the way, but those failed as well. Albertsons once again entered the story with an attempt to go public in 2018 through a merger with Rite Aid. This time the spoilsports were Rite Aid shareholders who, in their infinite wisdom (or lack thereof), decided to vote down the deal. They were concerned about the tremendous amount of debt Albertsons would add to the Rite Aid balance sheet.

Albertsons not only managed to go public on its own but as of this writing is in the process of attempting to merge with another grocery mega-chain, Kroger (NYSE: KR), in a $24.6bn deal. The deal trades at a very wide spread of 39% as I write this, because of—you guessed it—regulatory concerns.

Unlike the Rite Aid example, all is usually not lost when a deal fails. Some companies end up striking a new deal after a failed merger, as with Front Yard Residential after its failed acquisition by Amherst Residential for $12.50 per share. A year later, Front Yard struck a deal at a higher price of $13.50 per share with Pretium and Ares Management. There have been instances where a new deal was struck just two weeks after the failure of a deal—Agnico Eagle acquired TMAC Resources at a 26% premium to the prior failed deal with China's Shandong Gold Mining Co.—and in other instances it took years for a new deal to materialize.

However, the real opportunity in failed deals is not the potential of a new suitor or the termination fee the company might collect but the forced selling that often follows a failure. Most arbitrage-focused funds will exit their position after a deal fails, and this often artificially depresses the stock of the target company for several days after failure.

Case study 2: Rogers

The Rite Aid example helped us understand how regulators like the FTC look at a deal. Our second case study looks at a situation where a regulator dragged their feet for so long that the acquiring company used the opportunity to get out of a deal that was no longer attractive to them.

There are few acronyms that strike more fear into an arbitrageur's heart than SAMR. The State Administration for Market Regulation (SAMR) is where deals often go to die. Just like the U.S. has the FTC, the UK has the Competition and Markets Authority (CMA) and Europe has the European Commission, China has SAMR. Each of these regulatory agencies is tasked with ensuring that there is enough competition in the markets under their jurisdiction and M&A activity does not result in monopolies.

If two U.S.-based companies are merging but have some operations in other countries, they are required to receive regulatory approval in those countries. The countries from which a deal requires approval are usually listed in the definitive merger agreement.

We saw earlier that SAMR ran out the clock on Qualcomm's acquisition of NXP Semiconductors (NXPI) by not making a decision on the acceptability of the deal. In that case Qualcomm was keen on completing the deal and kept extending the competition deadline. Not all acquirers are keen on extending the outside date of an agreement and waiting for SAMR to make a decision.

On October 2, 2021, DuPont de Nemours (NYSE: DD) announced a $5.2bn acquisition of fellow engineered material company Rogers (ROG) in an all-cash deal worth $277 per share. DuPont was keen on acquiring Rogers as it paid a premium of 46% to acquire the company.

Less than three months after the deal was announced, it sailed through U.S. antitrust approval. About a month later shareholders approved the deal. Eight long months after shareholder approval, the companies announced they had received all required regulatory approvals with the exception of SAMR. At the request of SAMR, DuPont withdrew and refiled the notice of the planned merger. About a month after that, nearly 13 months after the deal was announced, DuPont called off the merger indicating it had not received timely clearance from regulators. DuPont paid Rogers a $162.5m termination fee and Rogers' stock crashed more than $100 per share in a single day.

SAMR approvals can sometimes take anywhere from 12 to 15 months, and companies really need to be committed to a deal to see it through. In the case of DuPont, the macroenvironment changed significantly after the deal was inked. The world went from a low interest rate environment to some of the largest interest rate increases in decades in an attempt to bring inflation under control, and there were significant concerns of a recession if the U.S. Federal Reserve was unable to engineer a soft landing for the economy.

Deals gathering dust on SAMR's desks almost always trade with large spreads, which inevitably attracts arbitrage tourists. The large spread does not compensate for the brain damage or loss of sleep from watching a deal get delayed month after month with no visibility. The annualized returns also take a hit even if the deal does eventually close. Experienced arbitrageurs avoid deals with significant cross-border risk as well as deals in the banking, insurance and utility sectors. Banking, insurance and utility deals require approval from other regulators or local jurisdictions they operate in.

The rebound trade

Not all failures are created equal, and it is best to analyze failed deals before choosing to get into a technical rebound trade. I invested in Rogers during the attempted acquisition by DuPont, then made money on the expected rebound in the stock after all the forced selling was over. Despite the trade working out well for me in a short period of time, I got into it early and was early exiting the trade. Waiting a few days to get in and waiting even longer to get out would have significantly enhanced my returns.

The massive $34.45bn acquisition of Willis Tower Watson (NASDAQ: WTW) by the insurance giant AON PLC (NYSE: AON) fell apart in mid-2021 and provided a similar opportunity post-failure, but the rebound was much faster than the Rogers situation (as you can see in Image 2.5).

Image 2.5: Willis Tower Watson (WTW) stock price chart

Source: InsideArbitrage.com

Hepatitis C is a viral infection transmitted through contact with blood that can cause liver inflammation and, in some cases, serious liver damage. Until a drug called Sovaldi was approved by the FDA in December 2013, there was no cure for the infection and patients had to both live with a chronic disease and risk transmitting it to others.

Pharmasset, the company developing Sovaldi, was running phase 3 trials when biotech giant Gilead Sciences (GILD) decided to acquire it for a whopping $11bn. Considering Gilead only had a market cap of $30bn when the deal was struck in November 2011, investors were shocked that it was willing to bet $11bn on a company with just 82 employees and no marketable products.

Gilead paid an 89% premium to acquire Pharmasset, and this was after the stock had more than tripled in the prior year. Did this bold bet by Gilead pay off?

The bet not only paid off, it helped Gilead generate $25bn in revenue in a single year once the drug was approved. Demand for Gilead's hepatitis C drugs was soon off the charts, as a single three-month course cured patients.

The primary downside for the company was that, since the drug completely cured patients, there was no repeat business. The downside for patients was the exorbitant cost of the drug, which in the U.S. cost over $80,000 for a three-month course. The company came under fire for selling the drug for as little as $500 for a full course in certain emerging markets, while charging a very high price in developed countries.

When the acquisition of Pharmasset was announced by Gilead, investors did not know that Sovaldi would be approved, how long the approval might take, or how Gilead would price the drug. Gilead's stock dropped sharply after the deal was announced, and I have long regretted not buying the stock following the drop despite having followed the company for years.

This drop in an acquiring company's stock can be even more dramatic if the deal is an all-stock deal or a cash-plus-stock deal. Arbitrageurs have to short the stock of the acquiring company to capture the spread, and this can create temporary downward pressure on the acquiring company's stock. Just as we discussed temporary price dislocation in the target company after a deal fails, we can potentially benefit from a similar dislocation in the acquiring company's stock after a large deal is announced.

While these situations are not common, I have used them to illustrate how there are several ways to benefit from the merger arbitrage strategy. As you gain experience with the strategy, you can come up with your own unique ways to profit from it.

An alternative to bonds

Everyone likes to say, "buy low, sell high." While it makes logical sense that you want to buy something when it is a bargain and sell after it becomes expensive, any investor that has been investing for a while realizes that this is easier said than done. There is however a way for investors, on average, to buy low and sell high.

To explain how investors can do this, I am going to digress into explaining the role of bonds in portfolios and then see how merger arbitrage fits into the picture.

For decades, financial advisors used a 60/40 approach to managing their client's assets, where 60% of the portfolio was in stocks and 40% in bonds. This approach worked well because stocks and bonds were inversely correlated such that when one went up, the other went down.

A portfolio of this type would be rebalanced at periodic intervals, say every six months or once a year. Let us assume that an investor started out with $100,000, with $60,000 invested in stocks and $40,000 in bonds. Let us also assume that they had the good fortune of doing so during a raging bull market in which stocks were running up constantly, much to the delight of investors. At the end of six months, the portfolio's stocks would have appreciated 25%, to $75,000, while its bonds dropped to $35,000 (remember, they are often inversely correlated).

The total portfolio would then be worth $110,000. The financial advisor would sell down the stock portion of the portfolio to $66,000 and use that money to increase the bonds allocation to $44,000 to maintain the 60/40 ratio for this $110,000 portfolio.

This is a rule-based approach to the "buy low, sell high" advice that removes any emotion from the decision-making process. While it might not be the best decision in any given six-month period, over the long run it tends to work out well.

Bond investors, or debt investors, are for the most part risk averse, and preservation of capital is important for them even if it means smaller returns through interest payments on the debt. There are many flavors of bonds, including U.S. government bonds, corporate bonds, municipal bonds, and emerging market bonds.

There is one group of bonds that are further out on the risk spectrum. These are called high yield bonds, or junk bonds. Investors in these bonds are willing to take additional risk that the debt might not get paid in return for higher interest on the debt. Think of the difference between home loans that are backed by the home compared to credit card debt. The lender can sell the home and recoup some or all of the borrowed money in the event the homeowner stops paying the mortgage and defaults on the loan. Credit card companies don't have the same protection on credit card debt and hence the difference in interest rates for home loans and credit card debt.

Bonds have different maturities and different interest rates based on those maturities. If a bond has a 5% interest rate and matures in 10 years, investors in the bond get paid 5% interest per year for 10 years and at the end of those 10 years get their money back when the bond issuer pays back the debt.

Bonds can be sold on the secondary market before they mature. Let us assume that five years after you purchase a bond that pays 5% interest, you need the money and would like to sell the bond to another investor on the secondary market. If at that point interest rates have gone up and a bond with a five-year maturity has a 7% interest rate, the investor on the secondary market will expect you to sell your 5% bond at a discount. The bond you purchased at a $1,000 par value will have to sell for approximately $900.

The investor buying the bond will pick up 5% interest per year on the bond for the next five years and will get $1,000 back from the bond issuer when the bond matures, provided the issuer has not defaulted on the bond. In addition to the interest, the investor makes $100 in capital gains when the $900 bond they purchased matures at $1,000.

The 60/40 portfolio worked well because the bond market was in a multi-decade bull market. Bonds were hit hard in 2022 as interest rates started going up. The next few decades might not be as kind to the bond market as prior ones.

Merger arbitrage provides an excellent alternative to bond investing. Instead of getting hit during times of high interest rates, merger arbitrage offers better returns because spreads widen to take time value of money into account.

Arbitrageurs have to be compensated for not just the risk of the deal failing but also the money that is tied up that could have earned interest in a bank account or certificate of deposit.

Depending on how an arbitrage portfolio is constructed it can be set up to mimic some of the same characteristics of a bond portfolio without the interest rate risk.

An investor that chooses deals with large spreads is in many ways going out on the risk profile the same way a high-yield or junk bond investor does.

It is important to keep in mind that during times of crisis, almost all correlations go to one and previously uncorrelated assets can drop in unison.

The dark side of merger arbitrage

In 1961, the Canadian government wanted to forcibly acquire all the assets of British Columbia Power. Following a court battle, the two parties finally settled on a price of $22.20. At one point during this battle, British Columbia Power was trading at around $19, providing for an arbitrage spread of over $3 per share. Charlie Munger was so confident that the deal would close that he convinced Warren Buffett to build a large position in British Columbia Power. He also put all his money into that trade and even borrowed money to capture the spread on that deal.

The dark side of merger arbitrage comes from those 5% of deals that can blow up and leave a gaping hole in your portfolio. If a diversified strategy is adopted in which you invest in every deal announced, then the fact that historically 95% of all deals tend to close is encouraging. However in practice investors rarely invest in dozens of deals simultaneously. Like Mr. Munger, they tend to pick and choose which deals they will participate in. Even if your thesis going into one of these deals with a large spread is that you would not mind owning the stock should the deal fall apart, the underlying sector fundamentals could change.

I was invested in the acquisition of the regional bank First Horizon (NYSE: FHN) by The Toronto-Dominion Bank (NYSE: TD) in an all-cash $13.4bn deal valued at $25 per share. When the deal was announced, First Horizon was the 37th largest bank in the United States with nearly $89bn in assets. The spread on the deal started out small and then grew to over 20%, providing for a good arbitrage opportunity. Over time, as it looked like the banks would receive regulatory approval, the spread narrowed to less than 1%, providing a good exit for arbitrageurs that did not want to wait right until the deal closed.

Waiting for that last 1% proved to be very expensive, because in early 2023 the U.S. banking industry was hit with several large bank failures including that of Silicon Valley Bank, which sent shockwaves throughout the industry. First Horizon and TD decided to call off their merger and the stock of First Horizon dropped sharply to under $10 per share, a far cry from the $25 that TD had been willing to pay for the company.

Unfortunately for investors that are just discovering the merger arbitrage strategy, the deals with small spreads but a high probability of closing are not all that attractive. The concept of annualized returns is not internalized, and a small 3% spread that can be captured in three months is not enticing. They tend to gravitate towards deals with large spreads and take on significant risk. They might not have the background in law that Mr. Munger had to determine the probability of British Columbia Power winning in court.

Institutional investors with a long track record of success in merger arbitrage often have a mix of deals with small and large spreads but take steps to hedge the risks on large deals by using options.

The dark side of merger arbitrage comes both from the risk of deal failure and from starting an arbitrage position with the intention of holding on to it if the deal fails, without regard for changing macroeconomic conditions.

Bringing it all together

To summarize our chapter on merger arbitrage:

1. When a company merges with another company or is acquired by a larger company, the stock of the target company rarely trades at the acquisition price, leaving a small spread for arbitrageurs to capture.

2. The reasons the spread exists can include the risk that the shareholders of the company might reject the deal, the risk that the acquiring company is unable to raise money for the deal and the risk that

regulators might reject the deal. This is the reason merger arbitrage is also known as risk arbitrage. The arbitrageur is taking on the risk that the deal might not close.

3. Arbitrageurs focus on annualized returns. If a deal offers a profit of just 4% but closes in 4 months, this is the equivalent of an annualized return of 12%. The arbitrageur does need to find other deals that offer similar returns once the first one closes. This does not include compounding of capital, which can push the annual returns a little higher.

4. Deals can be all cash, all stock, a combination of cash plus stock or special conditions deals. Arbitrageurs often prefer all-cash deals because capturing the spread in an all-stock or cash-plus-stock deal requires shorting the stock of the acquiring company.

5. Nearly 95% of deals announced between 2010 and 2022 ended up closing despite this period including the Covid-19 pandemic when the number of failed deals spiked higher.

6. While failed deals can deliver a large loss to an arbitrageur as the target company drops down to the pre-acquisition price or even lower, there is also upside in the strategy from deals that end up in bidding wars.

7. Stocks of companies that have experienced a deal break tend to sell off sharply as event-driven funds unload their holdings rapidly. These companies could provide short-term opportunities as a rebound play once the forced selling is done.

8. A definitive merger agreement is very difficult to get out of once signed. An acquirer that attempts to walk away has to often face a lawsuit from the target company and these lawsuits are more often than not settled out of court as we saw with Elon Musk's acquisition of Twitter.

9. There are several creative ways to express a merger arbitrage strategy by using options.

10. Some investors like to use merger arbitrage as an alternative to bonds, especially during times when interest rates are low and bond yields are unattractive.

CHAPTER 3

INSIDER TRANSACTIONS

I N INVESTING, STAYING within your circle of competence can be tremendously valuable. Opportunities within that circle are often those where you have an edge over the market. One of the reasons for the spectacular failure of the fund Long-Term Capital Management, as detailed in the book *When Genius Failed* by Roger Lowenstein, was their decision to stray outside their circle of competence.

Investing in biotech companies is outside my circle of competence, and I have no edge in analyzing which products in a company's pipeline are likely to succeed, how they are positioned compared to competitors and the potential market opportunity even if the drug is approved by the FDA. I often reach out to a group of friends that have Ph.Ds in neuroscience, cancer immunology and molecular biology to help me understand certain opportunities. Despite their sage advice, I tend to come away thinking I am attempting to read tea leaves.

There are always exceptions to rules, and an exception I like to make with biotech companies is where the company already has approved products, the financials make sense and most importantly an insider is buying stock on the open market. The specific kind of insider I am looking for is either a founder of the company or an independent director that has been on the board of directors for a long time.

Vertex Pharmaceuticals showed up on my radar during the depths of the pandemic in November 2020 when an independent director, Bruce Sachs, purchased 15,000 shares at an average price of $217.36 for $3.26m. Nearly 12 years had elapsed since Mr. Sachs' last purchase of Vertex during the Great Recession in 2008. Clearly this was an opportunistic purchase, and insider buying at Vertex was rare. The only insider purchase before his had occurred eight years earlier.

At the time of his purchase, Mr. Sachs had been serving on Vertex's board for nearly 22 years. He had also been a general partner at early-stage venture capital firm Charles River Ventures (CRV) for 21 years. CRV was founded in 1970 to commercialize research that came out of MIT.

The money shot was however when a subscriber, who received an alert about the Vertex insider transaction from InsideArbitrage, reached out to me and gave me some background about Mr. Sachs. He mentioned that Mr. Sachs was not only smart, he was know for being extremely hardworking. In the 1990s, when Mr. Sachs went home during the weekends, he would often take along two briefcases worth of work to pore over during the weekend.

While this anecdote about Mr. Sachs was fascinating, it was not sufficient to qualify Vertex for an investment. It is always best to do your own due diligence and see if a company is suitable. Vertex Pharmaceuticals is a biotechnology company that focuses on therapies for cancer, pain, inflammatory diseases, influenza, and other rare diseases. The company has multiple approved medicines that treat the underlying cause of cystic fibrosis (CF).

Cystic fibrosis is a progressive, genetic disease that causes persistent lung infections and limits the ability to breathe over time. The company's CF line of drugs was driving both revenue growth and profitability for the company even as it rapidly expanded its pipeline of therapies for diseases such as sickle cell disease, beta thalassemia, Duchenne muscular dystrophy and type 1 diabetes mellitus.

Despite a challenging market environment, during the two years since Mr. Sachs' purchase, Vertex was up nearly 40%, outperforming the S&P 500 by over 50%. Over the years I have watched the company execute well, including its partnership with CRISPR Therapeutics (NASDAQ: CRSP) to use gene editing to develop new therapies. Vertex has remained a core holding in my personal portfolio.

You have probably heard of the saying attributed to Peter Lynch: "Insiders might sell their shares for any number of reasons, but they buy them for only one: they think the price will rise."

Mr. Lynch, the famous manager of the Fidelity Magellan Fund, delivered returns of 29% a year for his investors over a 13-year period from 1977 to 1990, and wrote the book *One Up On Wall Street*. To put his performance in perspective, he doubled his investors' money every three years and many early investors in his fund went on to become multi-millionaires.

Mr. Lynch got the selling part of his quote on insiders right, but he is only partially right when it comes to insider buying. Before I get into why Mr. Lynch is only partially right, let me first define who company insiders are and what is classified as an insider transaction.

Who are company insiders?

An insider is any member of the company's management team including the C-suite (CEO, CFO, etc.) all the way down to the VP level. Members of the board of directors including the chair of the board are also insiders.

Anyone who owns more than 10% of the company's stock, even if they are not on the board, is also considered an insider. This means that if a fund builds a position in a company and crosses the 10% threshold, it is now classified as an insider.

All insiders are required to file a form called the Form 4 with the SEC after every purchase or sale of the company's stock. For example, when Berkshire Hathaway (NYSE: BRK.A) added to its position in HP (NYSE: HPQ) and Occidental Petroleum (NYSE: OXY), Berkshire had to file Form 4s, as you can see in Image 3.1.

In another example, when Dan Loeb's hedge fund Third Point sold shares of Upstart Holdings (NASDAQ: UPST) in December 2021 and SentinelOne (NYSE: S) in April 2022, it had to file Form 4s for each of these sales.

When an insider buys shares on the open market, sells shares, exercises options, gifts shares to someone, participates in a secondary offering by the company, converts shares from one class to another, etc., they have to file a Form 4 with the SEC.

Insiders can sometimes suffer from the same biases that you and I do. They might be anchored to a higher price and believe that just because a stock has dropped significantly, it is cheap and makes for a great investment. Considering how deeply insiders are embedded in their company's operations, they might have tunnel vision and fail to see the broader picture. Changes in the macroenvironment or industry-specific headwinds get picked up relatively quickly by markets, but insiders might be slow to realize these shifts are occurring.

I reached this conclusion intuitively by observing the behavior of insiders and the subsequent performance of companies after an insider purchase. There is also academic research on this phenomenon in a paper called "Do Managers Always Know Better? The Relative Accuracy of Management and Analyst Forecasts" by Amy Hutton, Lian Fen Lee and Susan Z. Shu. I discuss the paper and its conclusions in more detail in the chapter about stock buybacks.

Image 3.1: Berkshire Hathaway's Form 4 filing for the purchase of HP

SEC Form 4

FORM 4

☐ Check this box if no longer subject to Section 16. Form 4 or Form 5 obligations may continue. See Instruction 1(b).

UNITED STATES SECURITIES AND EXCHANGE COMMISSION
Washington, D.C. 20549

STATEMENT OF CHANGES IN BENEFICIAL OWNERSHIP

Filed pursuant to Section 16(a) of the Securities Exchange Act of 1934
or Section 30(h) of the Investment Company Act of 1940

1. Name and Address of Reporting Person*			2. Issuer Name and Ticker or Trading Symbol HP INC [HPQ]	5. Relatio (Check al
BERKSHIRE HATHAWAY INC				
(Last)	(First)	(Middle)	3. Date of Earliest Transaction (Month/Day/Year) 04/04/2022	
3555 FARNAM STREET				
(Street)	NE	68131	4. If Amendment, Date of Original Filed (Month/Day/Year)	6. Individ
OMAHA				X
(City)	(State)	(Zip)		

Table 1 - Non-Derivative Securities Acquired, Disposed of, or Beneficially Owned

1. Title of Security (Instr. 3)	2. Transaction Date (Month/Day/Year)	2A. Deemed Execution Date, if any (Month/Day/Year)	3. Transaction Code (Instr. 8)		4. Securities Acquired (A) or Disposed Of (D) (Instr. 3, 4 and 5)		
			Code	V	Amount	(A) or (D)	Price
Common Stock	04/04/2022		P		4,391,884	A	$36.4346[1]
Common Stock	04/05/2022		P		2,388,227	A	$36.2222[6]
Common Stock	04/06/2022		P		4,104,113	A	$34.8803[7]
Common Stock	04/06/2022		P		249,341	A	$35.5495[8]

Source: U.S. Securities and Exchange Commission

Sometimes you will notice that more than one insider at a company is buying shares at the same time. These types of purchases are different from the same insider buying shares multiple times.

Insider purchases by multiple insiders of a company are commonly referred to as Cluster Purchases.

Cluster purchases

While it is encouraging to see a CEO or the chair of the board purchase shares multiple times, it is even better to see that more than one insider is buying shares. Cluster purchases show that multiple insiders are willing to invest their own money and hold a variant perception about the stock compared to market participants like you and I.

Rich Barton was a general manager at Microsoft in the 1990s when he pitched the idea for a travel website to Bill Gates and Steve Ballmer. Expedia was founded inside Microsoft and later spun off as a separate company with Mr. Barton as CEO. The company went public in 1999 and was acquired by IAC (NASDAQ: IAC) in 2003 for $3.64bn. This was not the only billion-dollar company that Rich Barton founded. A few years after the sale of Expedia to IAC, he went on to found the real estate website Zillow with its unique Zestimate feature that provided estimates of how much homes were worth even if they were not for sale. If founding two large companies within a decade was not enough, he went on to also co-found Glassdoor in 2007.

Mr. Barton joined Netflix's board of directors in 2002 and picked up over a half-million dollars' worth of Netflix (NASDAQ: NFLX) shares for his personal portfolio on April 25, 2012. He held on those shares and saw his position appreciate more than 1,600% over the next 10 years, despite a huge drop in the stock in recent years. Just days after his purchase, another board member, Jay Hoag, also purchased shares. We discuss his purchase in more detail in a case study later in this chapter. Cluster purchases by company insiders and especially purchases by independent directors can be a strong signal for investors.

Now that you understand who company insiders are and how some of them tend to purchase shares in clusters, I will outline specific things you should keep an eye out for that will help you benefit from tracking insider purchases.

Strategies to benefit from insider purchases

There have been several academic studies over the years exploring the outperformance of insider trades and specifically insider buying. These studies have analyzed data over several decades and have shown that insider buying tends to outperform the overall market by 6.0% to 10.2% per year, depending on which academic study and time period you look at.

According to a Wharton study titled "Estimating the Returns to Insider Trading" that looked at a comprehensive sample of insider transactions over 22 years from 1975–1996, about one quarter of these abnormal returns accrue within the first five days after the trade and one half accrues within the first month.

You are likely to run into three key issues if you attempt to capture these excess returns.

1. There are thousands of insider transactions filed every year, and attempting to capture those returns would require investing in several hundred, or even a thousand, stocks.

2. Many of these stocks could be small or illiquid with low trading volumes that would make it hard to build a meaningful position.

3. Trading costs could take a bite out of returns if you have to buy hundreds or thousands of stocks. With most brokers now offering free trades, this is less of an issue these days.

It is well established that most of the signal in insider transactions comes from insider purchases and not from sales. In the current day and age of algorithmic and high-frequency trading, the opportunity to capture the early returns referenced in the Wharton study are likely gone. Investors can however benefit from well-informed insiders' variant perceptions over the long term.

Observe multiple companies in a single industry

It helps to pay attention to what insiders of multiple companies in the same industry are doing. Are the insiders of both Six Flags (NYSE: SIX) and Cedar Fair (NYSE: FUN) buying stock at the same time? Are the insiders of regional banks Zions Bancorporation (NASDAQ: ZION) and Huntington Bancshares (NASDAQ: HBAN) buying shares at the same time? Have oil company insiders, both large and small, started buying shares at increasingly higher prices?

When the entire market or a specific sector of the market is in trouble, investors generally shy away from making bold new investments. After all, who wants to run into a burning building even if there are valuables inside? We sometimes observe this with insiders, and watching their behavior can be quite instructive.

Futures are financial instruments that allow producers of commodities like corn and wheat to sell their commodities at a predetermined price in the future to a person or a company that plans to use that commodity at a later date. For example, a group of farmers might want to lock down the price of the corn they plan to plant so they know that they can sell it eight weeks later at a specified price. That way any fluctuations in the price of corn between planting and harvesting will not hit their profits come harvest time.

Who is the buyer of these futures? A cereal manufacturer like Kellogg Company (NYSE: K) might want to lock in the price of the corn it would need to produce its cereals and could be on the other side of the futures trade. Once this futures contract is in place, Kellogg will have to take delivery of the corn from the farmers on the expiration date. They can also sell the futures on an exchange like the Chicago Mercantile Exchange to speculators that buy and sell futures with no intention of taking delivery of the underlying commodity. Futures are not only limited to agricultural commodities like corn, wheat and soybeans. You can also buy futures for live cattle, milk, crude oil, natural gas, gold, copper, currencies, interest rates and a whole lot more.

The global lockdowns we saw in the early months of the Covid-19 pandemic hit commodity markets hard and especially the energy industry. The April 2020 swoon in energy prices, which at one point saw West Texas Intermediate (WTI) crude oil futures dip into negative territory for the first time ever, roiled energy markets worldwide. The global benchmark Brent oil futures did not come close to the decline WTI futures experienced, but most energy companies were hit hard by the Covid-19 related collapse in demand and the sudden drop in oil futures.

The negative price of WTI crude oil was primarily on account of the fact that anyone holding WTI futures was required to take delivery of oil at Cushing, Oklahoma if they didn't sell those futures before the expiry date. Since most speculators trading futures have no intention of taking physical delivery of any commodity, they usually settle the trade before expiry. In this case, there were no buyers and hence traders were willing to sell their futures at a negative price to get out of the contract and avoid taking delivery in Cushing, Oklahoma.

Harold Hamm, the founder and CEO of oil production company Continental Resources started buying shares on the open market on June 23, 2020 and over the course of the next two weeks acquired 10.55m shares worth $178m at an average price of $16.87. Following these purchases, he owned 81% of the total shares outstanding. Harold Hamm felt so strongly about just how undervalued Continental Resources was that he took the unusual step to announce his purchases through a press release where he stated:

I firmly believe Continental's current share price reflects an uncommon value as the global pandemic has negatively impacted worldwide crude oil demand. Recent purchases underscore my confidence in the Company's continued operational excellence and strong financial performance. Continental is poised to deliver significant shareholder value for many years to come and I believe there is no management team more aligned with shareholders than Continental.

Harold Hamm kept adding to his stake in Continental Resources over the next two years and eventually took the company private by acquiring the shares he didn't already own for $74.28 per share in cash, more than 340% above his purchases in June 2020. Investors had multiple opportunities to participate in the upside in Continental Resources. They could have followed Harold Hamm's lead and purchased shares after his insider purchase or, if they wanted a better/risk reward opportunity, participated in the merger arbitrage situation after he made his offer to take the company private.

I was invited to submit an idea to Seeking Alpha's "Marketplace Roundtable" in mid-2022 and I wrote the following when I submitted Continental Resources as my idea:

> One special situation that looks very interesting at the moment is the bid by the founder and executive chairman of Continental Resources to take the company private for $70 per share in cash. The stock currently trades at $65.05. Mr. Hamm and his family already own 83% of the stock and it's unlikely that another bidder will emerge but it is possible that Mr. Hamm could sweeten the deal a little to convince the board. If the deal goes through, it provides a return of 7.6% in a short period of time. The annualized return works out to more than 22% if the deal closes in 4 months.

The situation worked out even better when Mr. Hamm had to increase the price he offered for Continental Resources to $74.28 per share in cash. I participated in this pre-merger situation and my stock was eventually acquired. The only reason I did not buy Continental Resources earlier was because I already had an oversized allocation to the energy sector through holdings in oil pipeline companies and another fracking company.

Mr. Hamm was not the only energy company insider buying shares, and I saw broad-based buying across that industry. I saw something similar with regional bank insiders in March 2023 following the failure of Silicon Valley Bank in the span of two days. Silicon Valley Bank was the 16th largest bank in the U.S. with $209bn in assets as of December 31, 2022. The FDIC took control of the bank and eventually sold it to First Citizens Bank (NASDAQ: FCNCA).

So what happened to trigger this sudden collapse? In three words, a crisis of confidence. The bank made two announcements without thinking through the second-order effects of those announcements.

It indicated that it was selling substantially all of its available-for-sale securities portfolio for $21bn and taking a loss of $1.8bn in Q1 2023. Then it attempted to raise additional capital through a secondary offering. Venture capital firms, private equity firms and their portfolio companies immediately started withdrawing cash, leading to a crisis of confidence and the eventual collapse of the bank. It was a modern-day digital run on a bank that saw its stock price go from $267 to $0 in the span of two days.

It did not help that another bank, Silvergate Capital, had failed earlier the same week. Signature Bank of New York failed two days after Silicon Valley Bank.

The longer explanation involves delving into asset-liability mismatch, bonds held to maturity, mark-to-market accounting and more that is beyond the scope of the topic at hand.

A joint statement released by the Treasury, Federal Reserve and FDIC about making the depositors of Silicon Valley Bank and Signature Bank whole helped alleviate some of the concerns investors had that other dominoes were likely to fall in the coming weeks.

Unfortunately, shareholders and bondholders of the failed banks did not benefit from these actions. The Monday following the failure of these banks, most regional bank stocks were in free fall. However, the contagion was contained and we didn't see cascading failures of multiple banks. This is when insiders of regional banks stepped in and started buying aggressively.

There are hundreds of publicly traded regional and community banks in the U.S. Insider transactions can help us narrow down the potential investments to explore, just like we saw with the energy industry crisis three years before the banking crisis.

Whether it is energy or banking, when you see an industry in crisis and insiders start buying in a frenzy, pay close attention. Investors in a state of short-term panic will likely throw out the baby with the bathwater. These are times when picking up the strongest companies in the industry can turn out to be very profitable. Take your time to do your due diligence and don't rush to buy at the first sign of trouble.

Are company directors also investment professionals?

Another thing I look for in insider transactions is whether an independent director of the company is buying shares and if this independent director is an investment professional. A director who is an investment professional has a deep understanding of the company and also knows how to value a company. Jay Hoag's purchase of Netflix and Bruce Sachs' purchase of the biotech company Vertex Pharmaceuticals are both examples of independent directors with an investment background purchasing shares.

The length of time an independent director has been involved with a company can also make a difference. For example, Mr. Sachs has served on Vertex's board since 1998. Similarly Rich Barton has been on Netflix's board since 2002.

The chair of the board

I also like to pay attention to the chair of the board, especially if they are an executive chair in a cyclical business and have observed how the business performs across multiple cycles. For example, Germán Larrea Mota-Velasco's purchases of Southern Copper (NYSE: SCCO) in 2015 were spot-on. He picked up shares of this global copper producer at prices ranging from $24.10 to $27.14 during a three-month period in the second half of 2015 as you can see in Image 3.2. The price of copper at that time had dropped below $2.40 per pound, the lowest it had been since the depths of the Great Recession. With the eventual rebound in the price of copper, Mr. Mota-Velasco started selling shares at prices that ranged from $39.44 all the way up to $82 per share.

Founders at the helm

Founders at the helm that are buying shares in their company are also interesting. For example, Joe Kiani's purchases of medical devices company Masimo (NASDAQ: MASI) nearly a decade ago were spot-on. For a more recent example, CEO Tim Chen's purchases of Nerdwallet (NASDAQ: NRDS) looked interesting.

Summary

To summarize, you should look for and track the following types of insider purchases:

- Multiple companies from the same industry,
- Cluster buying within a company,
- Long-serving independent directors,
- Chair of the board that has seen multiple cycles,
- Founder CEOs.

Image 3.2: Insider buying in Southern Copper (SCCO)

Owner	Relationship	Date	Transaction	Cost	# Shares	Value($)	Total Shares
ROCHA OSCAR GONZALEZ	President and CEO	Nov 27, 2015	Buy	$25.91	8,000	207,280	134,539
VELASCO GERMAN LARREA MOTA	Chairman of the Board	Nov 20, 2015	Buy	$27.14	334,000	9,064,894	2,870,567
VELASCO GERMAN LARREA MOTA	Chairman of the Board	Nov 19, 2015	Buy	$26.86	54,000	1,450,440	2,536,567
VELASCO GERMAN LARREA MOTA	Chairman of the Board	Nov 18, 2015	Buy	$26.17	112,000	2,931,264	2,482,567
VELASCO GERMAN LARREA MOTA	Chairman of the Board	Nov 12, 2015	Buy	$26.30	105,000	2,761,385	2,370,567
VELASCO GERMAN LARREA MOTA	Chairman of the Board	Nov 11, 2015	Buy	$26.64	30,000	799,080	2,265,567
VELASCO GERMAN LARREA MOTA	Chairman of the Board	Nov 10, 2015	Buy	$26.79	90,000	2,411,469	2,235,567
VELASCO GERMAN LARREA MOTA	Chairman of the Board	Nov 09, 2015	Buy	$26.70	75,000	2,002,875	2,145,567
VELASCO GERMAN LARREA MOTA	Chairman of the Board	Sep 29, 2015	Buy	$25.87	122,600	3,171,466	2,070,567
VELASCO GERMAN LARREA MOTA	Chairman of the Board	Sep 28, 2015	Buy	$25.75	27,400	705,619	1,947,967
VELASCO GERMAN LARREA MOTA	Chairman of the Board	Aug 26, 2015	Buy	$24.10	50,000	1,204,945	1,920,567
VELASCO GERMAN LARREA MOTA	Chairman of the Board	Aug 24, 2015	Buy	$25.07	250,000	6,268,250	1,870,567

Source: InsideArbitrage.com

I see insider purchases as an idea discovery tool. Following insiders cannot replace deep research needed to understand the company and the investment opportunity. I use it as one data point in my research and appreciate its ability to serve up companies I might have otherwise missed.

Low-signal insider transactions

Just like it is important to understand which types of insider transactions generate the highest signal, it is also necessary to weed out insider transactions that provide very little useful information.

While reviewing insider activity each weekend, I look for these kinds of transactions and exclude them when reporting the top five largest insider purchases and sales from the prior week.

The kinds of transactions that I exclude are:

- A cluster of insider purchases where it looks like all the insiders purchased shares at the exact same price. This indicates that the insiders were either participating in a secondary offering, reinvesting dividends paid by the company, or purchased shares through a retirement plan administered by the company. Reading the footnotes of the filing or checking recent press releases provides some insight into why the cluster of insiders were all buying at the exact same price. We look at how you can access the footnotes of a filing later in this chapter.

- An insider purchase and a sale on the same day for the same number of shares and at the same price. This usually indicates that the insider is transferring shares from one account to another or from one person to another. Once again the footnotes of the filing are your friend in determining what is going on.

- Insider transactions filed several months or years late. This happens with surprising frequency and it is important to pay attention to the date of the transactions in the Form 4 filing. Any variant perception the insider held at the time of the transaction may not be as relevant if you find out about it months later.

- Insider purchases by new directors or management team members. Some companies require their new directors or management team to hold a certain number of shares at all times. The insiders of these companies might buy to fulfill this requirement.

- Regular annual purchases by an insider. Looking at the history of purchases can help you identify if the company requires its directors or management team to acquire a certain number of shares each year.

- Contractually required purchases. In a rather unusual arrangement in August 2022, the social media company Pinterest (PINS) stuck a clause in the employment contract of its new CEO Bill Ready that he had to buy $5m worth of common shares of Pinterest on the open market within 60 days of starting his employment. This purchase would then make him eligible for a $20m grant of restricted stock. This requirement aligns Mr. Ready's interests with shareholders, but if I had just relied on the Form 4 filing without reading the footnotes, I might have interpreted his insider purchase as a big show of confidence in Pinterest stock.

- Insider sales where the insider exercised options and immediately sold those shares right after the exercise.

- The vesting of restricted stock units (RSUs), which are granted at a price of $0 to employees, is a taxable event for most insiders. In order to avoid a huge tax bill when filing taxes, companies set up an automated sale process where a portion of the vested RSUs are sold for tax withholding purposes. These kinds of sales have a different transaction code (F) in the Form 4 filing, but might appear like sales on most websites that report insider sales. Some companies make a mistake when filing these kinds of insider transactions and put the wrong transaction code (S), making it look like an opportunistic sale instead of an automatic one to cover the tax implications of vested stock or options. The footnotes of these filings usually contain enough information to determine if the sale was opportunistic or automatic.

Aggregate insider transactions and the sell/buy ratio

While I mostly use insider purchases as an idea-generation tool, I was surprised to see in March 2020, during the depths of the Covid-19 pandemic, that aggregate insider buying could also provide a big-picture signal. Every weekend I calculate a ratio called the sell/buy ratio that looks at the aggregate insider selling across all companies during the prior week and divides it by aggregate insider buying across all companies during that week. You can freely download the history of aggregate insider purchases and sales for each week since 2012 at InsideArbitrage.com/SellBuyRatio.xlsx.

Insiders as a group almost always sell more stock than they buy. This makes sense because a large part of their compensation or net worth is in company stock and they sell constantly to diversify their assets. On the other hand, if they want to buy stock, they have to do so with their own money or, in the case of funds, with their investors' money.

Looking at the data in the InsideArbitrage database, over a 12-year period from August 2010 through July 2022, the average weekly sell/buy ratio was 30.10. In other words, every week, insiders tend to sell 30 times as much stock as they buy. If insiders purchased $100m worth of stock in a given week, they were likely to have sold $3bn worth of stock in that week.

The sell/buy ratio is unfortunately skewed by very large sales by certain insiders that could include the richest people on planet Earth scaling back their exposure, or a large fund liquidating a position. For example, Jeff Bezos sold $3.02bn worth of Amazon.com (AMZN) stock in a single week in November 2020. He had already sold $4.07bn worth of stock in February 2020 and an additional $3.13bn worth of stock in August 2020. In a similar vein, Elon Musk sold $8.52bn worth of Tesla (TSLA) stock in a single week in April 2022 to fund his purchase of Twitter (TWTR).

Mr. Musk was in the midst of a bitter court battle with Twitter to avoid closing the deal, but wanted the money in case he lost the case and was forced to close the deal by the Delaware Court of Chancery.

Considering the average sell/buy ratio over that 12-year period was skewed by large transactions, I looked at the median sell/buy ratio and found that the median was 19.03. In other words, insiders sell 19 times as much stock as they purchase each week.

March 2020 was a painful month with markets in free fall following the rapid spread of Covid-19 across the globe. At a time when very little was known about the virus, we had no visibility into the potential for a vaccine, governments across the world were instituting lockdowns and people were losing lives and livelihoods, there was one group of investors that were buying hand over fist. In over 10 years of tracking the sell/buy ratio, I had not once come across an instance of total insider buying in a given week exceeding insider selling. That changed during the second week of March 2020, when insiders purchased $682.88m of stock. Insider selling, which had been elevated until the prior week, also dropped to $668.52m. The sell/buy ratio dropped to 0.98, the lowest in nearly a decade.

The following week, the insiders did it once again. Insiders purchased $533.25m of stock compared to $470.58m of sales. The sell/buy ratio dropped even further to 0.88.

The March 2020 situation was unique because of the rapid drop in markets in a matter of days and the unprecedented stimulus measures that were undertaken by governments and central banks across the globe. The insiders that were buying hand over fist at that time probably had experienced several challenging market cycles, were aware of the reserves the company possessed to help them ride out a few challenging quarters or had taken immediate action to reposition their business to survive a global pandemic.

They saw the blood in the streets and acted by putting their own money to work in their own stocks. The CEO of Wells Fargo (NYSE: WFC) stepped up to purchase nearly $5m worth of stock in a single week. So did eight different insiders of Simon Property Group (NYSE: SPG), the largest mall operator in the United States. Insiders also stepped up their insider buying significantly in the last quarter of 2008 and the first months of 2009. They purchased shares right before the March 2009 bottom during the Great Recession.

Since insiders tend to be early and most bear markets last longer than the one we experienced in March 2020, it might make sense to add to existing positions or start new positions very gradually and spread trades out over weeks or months, at risk of missing the first leg of the eventual rebound.

Market timing is very challenging as you have to get both the exit and the eventual re-entry right. Peter Lynch once said: "Far more money has been lost by investors trying to anticipate corrections, than lost in the corrections themselves."

While I would not advocate using the sell/buy ratio as a market timing tool, it can provide valuable input at the extremes. It is not a panacea, but combined with other indicators it can be a helpful guide.

When looking at aggregate insider transaction data, it is important to remember that during earnings-related quiet periods you will see a dramatic drop off in both insider selling and insider buying activity. Earnings-related quiet periods are established by companies to prevent their insiders and sometimes all employees from trading before or right after quarterly earnings are released. The length of the quiet period differs from company to company, but you can normally expect it to kick in two weeks before the end of a quarter and last from one to three days after the release of quarterly earnings.

Short-swing profit rule and flip-floppers

Dan Shulman, the CEO of PayPal (NASDAQ: PYPL), joined eBay (NASDAQ: EBAY) just a few months before it spun out PayPal as an independent company in July 2015. PayPal's stock went on a tear and at one point was up more than 650% since the spinoff from eBay as you can see in the chart in Image 3.3. The stock reversed course in the second half of 2021 and the sell-off accelerated in early 2022. Mr. Shulman, who until December 2021 was a seller of PayPal stock, turned around and purchased nearly $1m worth of stock on the open market in early February 2022. He was not the only insider to buy stock that week and two directors, David Dorman and Frank Yeary, also joined him in buying $1m and $499,400 worth of stock respectively. I like to refer to insiders that were selling stock and then suddenly start buying as flip-floppers.

Image 3.3: PayPal performance July 2015 to September 2023

Source: InsideArbitrage.com

While the term flip-flopper has a negative connotation in politics, it can be an admirable quality to possess as an investor. The noted English economist John Maynard Keynes is purported to have said: "When the facts change, I change my mind. What do you do, sir?"

If your original thesis for investing in a company changes because of the company's performance, it would make logical sense to sell the position instead of holding out hope for a turnaround. The words "hope" and "turnaround" can be particularly harmful to the long-term returns of a portfolio.

While investors should embrace flip-floppers, the SEC does not hold the same opinion when it comes to corporate insiders. In fact Section 16(b) of the Securities Exchange Act of 1934 states that if a purchase and a sale (or a sale and a purchase) occur within a six-month period, the insider has to disgorge any profits back to the company. This is referred to as the Short-Swing Profit rule. The rule is used to discourage insiders from using the information they possess to make short-term profits.

Every once in a while, we come across insider transactions where the insider indicates that the transaction violates the Short-Swing Profit rule and that the insider is going to return any profits from the prior trade back to the company. Flip-flopping insiders are sending us a signal that they think the prevailing winds have changed and that they are willing to give up some short-term profits to make even more money down the road. Mr. Shulman's insider purchase of PayPal in February 2022 included a footnote in the filing that stated:

> The Reporting Person has agreed to voluntarily disgorge to the Issuer all statutory "profits" pursuant to Section 16(b) of the Securities Exchange Act of 1934, as amended, that resulted from the transactions reported herein.

Case study 1: Netflix

On July 12, 2011 the streaming media pioneer Netflix made an announcement that shocked their customers and investors on Wall Street.

The company that launched as a DVD-by-mail service during the height of the dot-com bubble in the late 1990s correctly anticipated that the future of content would be streaming, and that DVDs were going to gradually fade into oblivion. What the company did not anticipate was the big backlash from customers when they announced that they were going to split their business into two, with one company focused on delivering DVDs by mail and another that delivered streaming content. To make matters worse, Netflix decided to call their new DVD-focused company Qwikster.

Subscribers quickly came to the conclusion that this announcement amounted to a 60% increase in their subscription costs if they kept both the DVD by mail and the streaming plan. Netflix's hit series like *House of Cards* and *Orange is the New Black* were set to launch in 2013—still two years away—and there was little to anchor subscribers to the streaming service when this split was announced. In the ensuing months, Netflix lost hundreds of thousands of subscribers and by October 2011, when the company reported it had lost 800,000 subscribers, the stock had dropped sharply. After the dust settled, the stock had lost more than 75% of its value from the date of announcement through the end of 2011.

I used to review insider transactions filed with the SEC every night. I write about the largest insider purchases and sales at the end of the week on my website in a series of posts called Insider Weekends that I have been publishing continuously for over 12 years. A little less than a year after Netflix announced its disastrous plan, in one of my regular nightly reviews, I noticed a large opportunistic purchase by an insider. A member of Netflix's board of directors, Jay Hoag, picked up $25m worth of Netflix stock over a three-day period in May 2012.

Mr. Hoag purchased Netflix shares indirectly through Silicon Valley venture capital firm Technology Crossover Ventures (now known as TCV), a VC firm he co-founded in 1995. TCV first invested in Netflix in 1999 and then went on to invest several more times both before and after Netflix went public. Mr. Hoag joined Netflix's board of directors in 1999, and by the time he filed the insider purchase in 2012 he had been involved with the company for 13 years. Mr. Hoag's transaction had all the hallmarks of a high-signal insider purchase that you should look for as an investor, including:

- A long-serving board member who had seen the company navigate its way through the deep bear market in 2001–2003 and once again in 2007–2009.

- A high-growth company that made a strategic, but not fatal, mistake.

- An insider who was an independent board member with an investment background.

Image 3.4 shows the stock price of Netflix from 2012 through 2016, and the point at which Mr. Hoag and TCV purchased.

Much to the relief of investors, Netflix eventually abandoned the plan to spin off its DVD-by-mail business and the stock eventually went up tenfold, as you can see in Image 3.4. Unfortunately for TCV, it did not hold its full position through that entire 1,000%+ increase.

The other noteworthy thing that jumps out from the chart is that Netflix's stock did not begin its ascent right away. The stock plateaued and built a base for several months before breaking out and starting a huge run up. Insiders, like value investors, are often early to the party. The insights they possess are likely to play out over the duration of several months or quarters, and the strategy of observing insider purchases best aligns with the goals of long-term oriented investors.

Image 3.4: Netflix performance after Jay Hoag's insider purchase

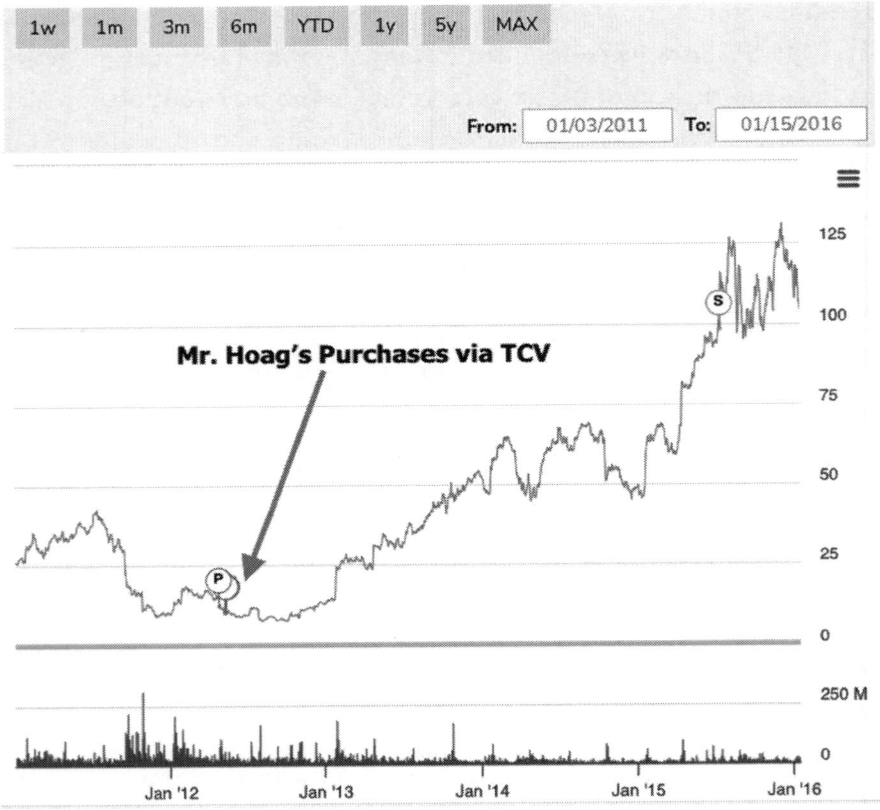

Source: InsideArbitrage.com

Insider selling

I have spent a lot of time discussing insider purchases but haven't discussed the implications of insider selling beyond the fact that aggregate insider selling is usually several times larger than insider buying. Management teams are often incentivized by large options or stock grants and over time these grants start to represent a larger portion of their compensation. This aligns the interests of management teams with those of shareholders. It also leads to insiders having a concentrated position in a single company.

While there are proponents of concentrated portfolios, most investors are better off with a diversified portfolio. Towards this end, it is not surprising to see that insiders are frequent sellers of their company stock, and this is all the more so for companies that are performing well with rising stock prices. During the bull market in technology stocks from 2016 to 2021, insider selling was dominated by tech company insiders. Taking this as a negative signal to sell a position or go short a stock would have caused significant damage to an investor's portfolio. Insider selling does not provide the same signal that insider buying does and this has been borne out by academic research over the decades.

So is there a time when you should pay attention to insider selling?

Elevated levels of aggregate insider selling across companies can signal trouble ahead. Insider selling also grabs my attention when I see a cluster of insiders selling shares simultaneously even as the stock price is declining. For this kind of selling to provide a meaningful signal, it has to be regular sales and not sales related to the exercising of options or the vesting of restricted stock units (RSUs). This kind of selling implies that the insiders are rushing for the exits while they still can and you should revisit your thesis for investing in the stock.

The first time I came across this pattern was in March 2011 when a mini bubble in solar energy had significantly driven up the price of companies like First Solar (NASDAQ: FSLR). The insiders started offloading several hundred million dollars' worth of stock in the span of a month at prices ranging from $139.85 per share to $156.77. A little more than a year later, in May 2012, the stock bottomed under $12 per share having lost more than 90% of its value.

Case study 2: Carvana

I saw this again in the case of online car dealership company Carvana (NASDAQ: CVNA). Car buying is rarely a pleasant experience for consumers, especially if said purchase happens at a car dealership. The initial excitement of taking home a new car often fades as you engage in a sales and financing process that often has more twists and turns than a Hitchcock thriller.

At the end of the ordeal, customers are often left wondering whether they really got what they walked in to buy. A few companies have attempted to solve this problem, including TrueCar (NASDAQ: TRUE), which lets you get firm quotes from various dealers before you show up at the dealership. Tesla (NASDAQ: TSLA) did the same thing with a streamlined online buying experience that included just a few steps and allowed you to pay the deposit for the car through a credit card.

Then there are the new-age, online-only dealers like Vroom, Shift and Carvana. There are other online marketplaces like Cars.com (NYSE: CARS), and CarGurus (NASDAQ: CARG), that like TrueCar facilitate sales by dealers. To stand out in this crowded but lucrative market, Carvana resorted to an innovative—some would say gimmicky—delivery method.

Customers who purchased a car online are sent a token. Once the car is ready, they go to their closest car vending machine. Yes, I said vending machine. The company built these attractive cylindrical towers that house cars. When a customer deposits a token, the vending machine identifies the car and after some impressive theatrics delivers the car to the customer.

The first few months of the pandemic shut down supply chains. A combination of stimulus money and savings from not commuting, eating out or traveling, left consumers with significant additional disposable capital. The M2 money supply is a measure used to track how much money consumers have including money in checking accounts, saving accounts, money market funds and certificates of deposits (CDs). As seen in Image 3.5, the M2 money supply shot up from $15.48bn at the start of 2020 to $21.72bn by the start of 2022, an unprecedented increase in a short period of time.

A combination of low inventory levels due to supply chain issues and extra money in consumer pockets led to a frenzy of car buying where used car prices started rising rapidly and new cars started selling well above the manufacturer's suggested retail price (MSRP). Gone were the days when car dealers offered discounts and deals to entice customers to buy cars.

In this environment, Carvana started offering very attractive prices to sellers of used cars. Carvana would quickly fix and refurbish these cars and then sell them on their platform. The excess cash sloshing around in customer accounts also found its way into the stock market. New investors that were there for their first rodeo started focusing on high-growth tech stocks and companies realized that their stocks were being rewarded for revenue growth and the bottom line did not matter.

Carvana was one of the beneficiaries of this phenomenon and saw its stock soar from around $30 at the bottom of the pandemic bear market in March 2020 to over $370 near the top in August 2021.

During the span of just two months in July and August 2021, a cluster of insiders unloaded more than $750m worth of Carvana stock at prices that at times exceeded $370 per share. Their timing was impeccable as Carvana started declining sharply shortly after this elevated level of insider selling.

Towards the end of 2021, investors came to their senses, and all of a sudden profitability started mattering again. This meant unprofitable companies like Carvana could not find a bottom. How do you value a company that perpetually posts losses and has negative free cash flow for nine years in a row?

The stock managed to lose nearly 95% of its value from a peak of $376.83 on August 10, 2021 to a trough of $19.83 on June 13, 2022. This precipitous drop triggered a cluster of insider buying by four different insiders at the company in June 2022. The stock then went on to more than double

Image 3.5: M2 money supply 2018–2023

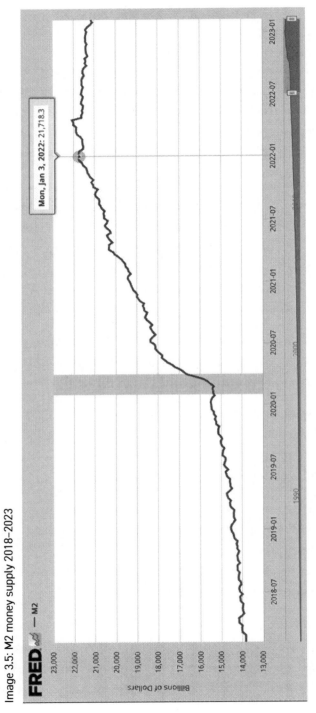

Source: Board of Governors of the Federal Reserve System (US)

from those levels and peaked at over $50 per share by August 16, 2022. The insiders of Carvana benefited both from selling near the top and then buying back after a huge correction in the stock price.

Unfortunately the second half of the story did not end as hoped for by the Carvana insiders as the stock dropped into the low single digits by December 2022. Beyond buying cars at elevated prices, Carvana also made a big mistake by buying KAR Global's car auction business for $2.2bn. The company attempted to raise cash for the deal through a secondary stock offering and also by issuing over $3bn in debt that appeared to have few takers. They finally managed to get the private equity giant Apollo Global to purchase half of that debt at a high interest rate of 10.25%. By the end of 2022 the company's net debt had ballooned to $7.2bn, not including capital leases, and the market was pricing the stock for bankruptcy.

When you see elevated selling by a group of company insiders, and if that selling continues when the stock price is in decline, pay special attention as the selling could signal trouble ahead.

Forced selling

Tracking forced selling by insiders or funds can also be useful in certain situations. The chair of the board or the CEO may be forced to sell a large amount of shares in a messy divorce, or a fund might choose to liquidate a large stake in the company.

I saw the latter in action when Japanese giant SoftBank sold its entire stake in Uber (NYSE: UBER) between April and July 2022. Uber's stock dropped to the low $20s during the period SoftBank was selling shares, significantly underperforming the Nasdaq. Once the overhang from forced selling or liquidations is complete, a stock is likely to rebound to a more natural level, driven by the company's valuation and investor perception of future growth. Forced selling provides you with an opportunity to pick up shares at an artificially low price, thereby setting you up to profit when the stock eventually rebounds.

Deconstructing a Form 4 filing

Insiders are required to file the Form 4 with the SEC within two business days of a transaction. They are required to file a Form 4 if they purchase shares, sell shares, gift shares to someone, exercise options or warrants, and even if they transfer shares from one account to another. If the company needs to raise more money by issuing new shares through a secondary offering and an insider participates in that offering, they have to file a Form 4 with the SEC. These might look like open market purchases because they use the same transaction code as a regular open market purchase.

To determine whether an insider purchase is an open market purchase or something else, it helps to go to the source of the information and look at the actual Form 4 filed with the SEC.

Every once in a while, I see insiders file a Form 4 several months or even several years late. It is important to look at the date of the transaction and not just the date of the Form 4 filing.

Sometimes insiders make mistakes in the transaction code they use in the Form 4 to indicate the transaction was a purchase when in fact it was a sale. These are sometimes corrected using an amended filing called a Form 4/A.

To help you understand the different components of a Form 4 filing, I have included a filing of Rich Barton's insider purchase of Netflix from 2012 in Images 3.6 to 3.10. Image 3.6 includes the full filing, and the four subsequent images include information about the various components of a Form 4 filing.

The top left of a Form 4 filing includes information about the name of the insider (included as last name followed by first name) and their address as seen in Image 3.7.

Image 3.6: Rich Barton's April 2012 purchase of Netflix

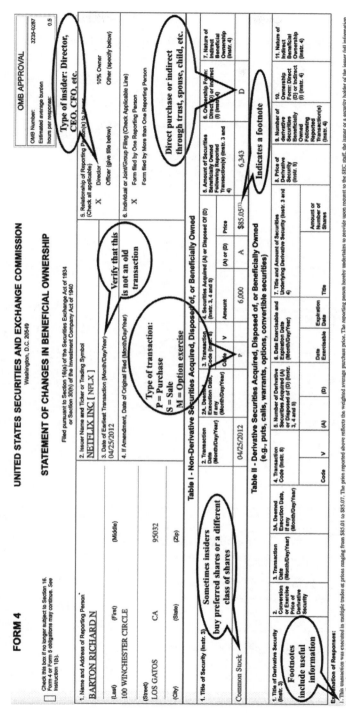

Source: U.S. Securities and Exchange Commission

The first part of the central section of a Form 4 called "Table I – Non Derivative Securities Acquired, Disposed of, or Beneficially Owned" gives you information about whether the filing is for common shares, preferred shares, or a specific class of shares. This information is important because of the price difference between preferred shares and common shares, as well as between different classes of common shares.

For example, the last trade for a class A share of Berkshire Hathaway was $429,819 September 9, 2022, while a class B share closed trading at $286 on the same day.

Image 3.7: Component 1 of Rich Barton's April 2012 purchase of Netflix

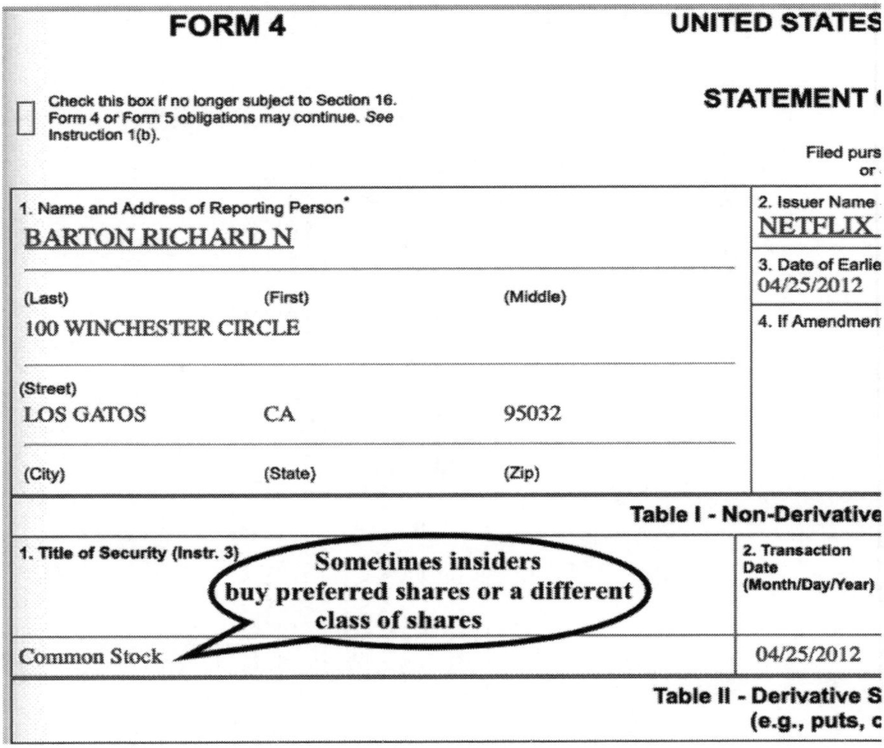

FORM 4

UNITED STATES

STATEMENT (

Check this box if no longer subject to Section 16. Form 4 or Form 5 obligations may continue. *See* Instruction 1(b).

Filed purs
or

1. Name and Address of Reporting Person*
BARTON RICHARD N
(Last) (First) (Middle)
100 WINCHESTER CIRCLE
(Street)
LOS GATOS CA 95032
(City) (State) (Zip)

2. Issuer Name
NETFLIX

3. Date of Earlie
04/25/2012

4. If Amendmen

Table I - Non-Derivative

1. Title of Security (Instr. 3)	2. Transaction Date (Month/Day/Year)
Common Stock	04/25/2012

Table II - Derivative S
(e.g., puts, c

Source: U.S. Securities and Exchange Commission

The top middle part of a Form 4 filing includes information about the name of the company, its ticker symbol, the date of the earliest transaction, and—if it is an amended Form 4 filing—the date of the original Form 4 filing as highlighted in image 3.8. A single Form 4 can contain information about multiple transactions and each of these transactions is represented as a separate row in the central section called "Table I – Non-Derivative Securities Acquired, Disposed of, or Beneficially Owned".

For each transaction in Table I, the "Transaction Code" column helps you understand if the transaction was a purchase (code P), a sale (code S), an options exercise (code M), payment of taxes related to an options exercise (code F), a gift (code G), etc.

Image 3.8: Component 2 of Rich Barton's April 2012 purchase of Netflix

UNITED STATES SECURITIES AND EXCHANGE COMMISSION
Washington, D.C. 20549

STATEMENT OF CHANGES IN BENEFICIAL OWNERSHIP

Filed pursuant to Section 16(a) of the Securities Exchange Act of 1934
or Section 30(h) of the Investment Company Act of 1940

2. Issuer Name and Ticker or Trading Symbol NETFLIX INC [NFLX]		5. R (Che
3. Date of Earliest Transaction (Month/Day/Year) 04/25/2012	*Verify that this is not an old transaction*	
4. If Amendment, Date of Original Filed (Month/Day/Year)	*Type of transaction:* *P = Purchase* *S = Sale* *M = Option exercise*	6. In

Table I - Non-Derivative Securities Acquired, Disposed of, or Beneficially Owned

2. Transaction Date (Month/Day/Year)	2A. Deemed Execution Date, if any (Month/Day/Year)	3. Transaction Code (Instr. 8)		4. Securities Acquired (A) or Disposed Of (D) (Instr. 3, 4 and 5)		
		Code	V	Amount	(A) or (D)	Price
04/25/2012		P		6,000	A	$85.05

Source: U.S. Securities and Exchange Commission

The top right of a Form 4 filing includes information about the type of insider that is filing the form, such as a 10% owner, director, CEO, CFO, VP of sales, etc. as seen in Image 3.9. If the title is too long to fit into this section, the title of the insider is included in the footnotes of the filing.

Table 1 in the middle section of the Form 4 also indicates whether the insider is buying shares directly for their account or indirectly for a spouse, for their children, through a trust, for their fund, or through a Limited Liability Company.

Image 3.9: Component 3 of Rich Barton's April 2012 purchase of Netflix

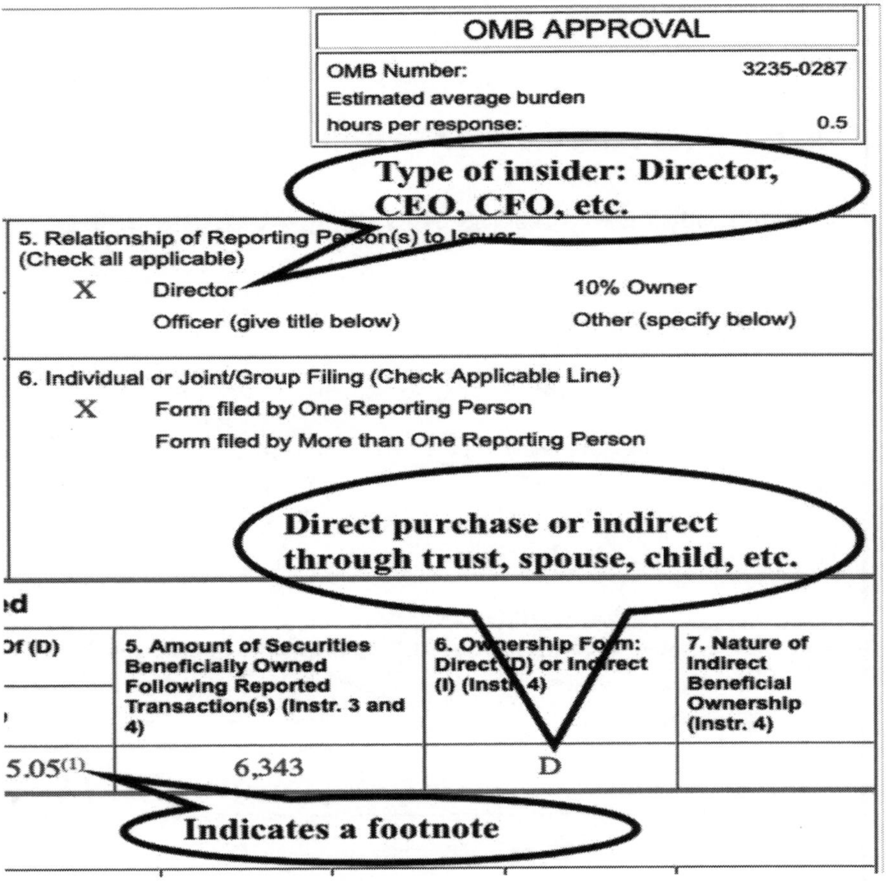
OMB APPROVAL

OMB Number: 3235-0287
Estimated average burden
hours per response: 0.5

5. Relationship of Reporting Person(s) to Issuer
(Check all applicable)
X Director
10% Owner
Officer (give title below)
Other (specify below)

6. Individual or Joint/Group Filing (Check Applicable Line)
X Form filed by One Reporting Person
Form filed by More than One Reporting Person

d

Of (D)	5. Amount of Securities Beneficially Owned Following Reported Transaction(s) (Instr. 3 and 4)	6. Ownership Form: Direct (D) or Indirect (I) (Instr. 4)	7. Nature of Indirect Beneficial Ownership (Instr. 4)
5.05[1]	6,343	D	

Source: U.S. Securities and Exchange Commission

Towards the bottom of the Form 4 filing, the insider includes information about derivative transactions in a section called "Table II – Derivative Securities Acquired, Disposed of, or Beneficially Owned". If a company has awarded its CEO four million options with one million of those options vesting every year for the next four years, information about when those options are exercisable, the exercise price, expiration date, etc., is included in Table II.

Immediately below Table II is an important area of the Form 4 filing in a section titled "Explanation of Responses," which includes the footnotes of the filing as highlighted in Image 3.10. Investors should pay special attention to the footnotes of SEC filings as they provide important context or explanations about the filing. Companies also sometimes bury information in the footnotes that they may not want investors to pay close attention to.

Form 4 filing footnotes can include information about whether a purchase transaction was through a secondary offering and the insider participated in the secondary offering. Insiders often participate in secondary offerings as a show of confidence. Every single one of Elon Musk's insider purchases of Tesla from 2012 to 2017 was related to him participating in secondary offerings instead of buying shares on the open market.

Image 3.10: Component 4 of Rich Barton's April 2012 purchase of Netflix

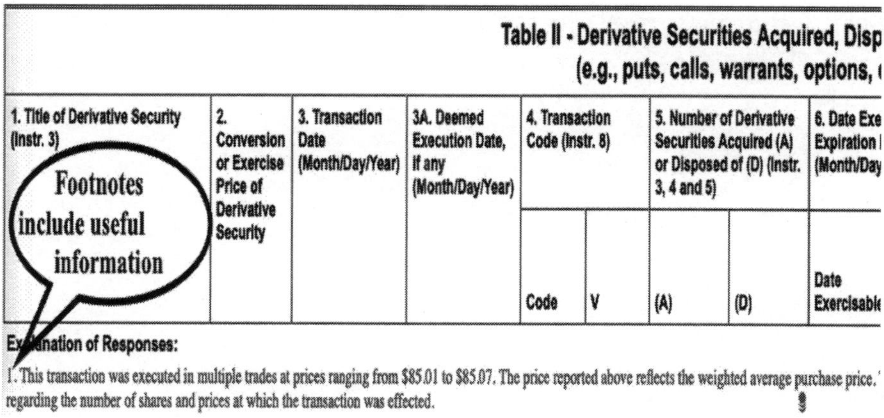
Table II - Derivative Securities Acquired, Disp
(e.g., puts, calls, warrants, options,

1. Title of Derivative Security (Instr. 3)	2. Conversion or Exercise Price of Derivative Security	3. Transaction Date (Month/Day/Year)	3A. Deemed Execution Date, if any (Month/Day/Year)	4. Transaction Code (Instr. 8)		5. Number of Derivative Securities Acquired (A) or Disposed of (D) (Instr. 3, 4 and 5)		6. Date Exe Expiration (Month/Day
				Code	V	(A)	(D)	Date Exercisabl

Explanation of Responses:

1. This transaction was executed in multiple trades at prices ranging from $85.01 to $85.07. The price reported above reflects the weighted average purchase price.
regarding the number of shares and prices at which the transaction was effected.

Source: U.S. Securities and Exchange Commission

Accessing Form 4 filings

Now that you know how to read a form 4 filing, let us address where you can find them. When it comes to financial information of any kind, it is often best to go to the source of the information. The SEC allows you to pull up all filings by a company (not just the Form 4 filings) from its EDGAR system: www.sec.gov/edgar/search.

Image 3.11: SEC EDGAR search

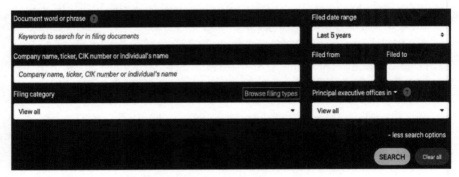

Source: U.S. Securities and Exchange Commission

Using EDGAR, enter the name of the company you are interested in or its ticker symbol, select the filing category as "Insider equity awards, transactions, and ownership (Section 16 Reports)," and click on the search button to pull up the insider filings for that company. For example, Image 3.12 shows the Form 4 filings for Apple (NASDAQ: AAPL).

Image 3.12: Form 4 results for Apple (AAPL) from EDGAR

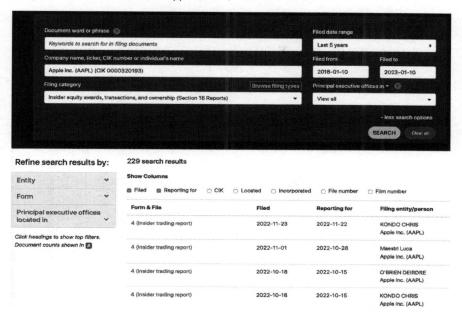

Source: U.S. Securities and Exchange Commission

The SEC also makes this information freely available in a format that can be easily consumed by computers. Websites like InsideArbitrage.com and others use this information to capture Form 4 data and make it accessible to investors in a format that makes it very easy to review. Investors can view multiple Form 4 filings together without having to open them one by one. Image 3.13 shows insider purchases for companies with a stock price of $5 and over. The list has also been filtered to eliminate any purchases that are less than $5,000 in value.

Image 3.13: Insider purchases

Source: InsideArbitrage.com

The dark side of insider transactions

Insiders are aware that market participants pay attention to insider transactions and sometimes you see insiders purchase stock just to signal the market. This is an example of George Soros's theory of reflexivity in action.

In a few cases, the company may go so far as to issue a press release to draw attention to the insider transaction, which under normal circumstances should be a big red flag for you. A notable exception to this was Harold Hamm's insider purchase of Continental Resources discussed earlier in this chapter. The timing of that purchase was excellent, despite the issuance of a press release. As indicated in that press release, the transaction was part of a "10b5-1 plan."

On October 2000, the SEC adopted new rules including Regulation FD and rule 10b5-1. Regulation FD (Fair Disclosure) prohibits companies from disclosing material information to investors including but not limited to institutions, portfolio managers or analysts, if that information is not already known by the general public. Information is deemed material if it can move the price of a company's stock or can be important enough to impact an investor's decision to buy or sell a stock.

In other words, having easy access to key insiders in a company should not provide investors with an unfair advantage compared to the general public. Insiders of a company are likely to know about material information including quarterly earnings, new discoveries, a drug approval, a large customer contract, etc., before most investors.

If an insider wants to buy or sell stock over a period of time and does not want to be implicated for insider trading while in possession of material non-public information, they can set up a 10b5-1 plan. A 10b5-1 plan outlines the price, amount and dates of trades, and gives the broker that executes the trades the ability to determine when to make the purchases or sales. Insiders are supposed to set up these plans before they come into possession of material non-public information.

The footnotes of Form 4 filings usually indicate whether a transaction was part of a 10b5-1 plan. Insiders do have some flexibility in setting up and canceling these plans, and these plans are subject to being gamed. In fact, the predecessor to the 10b5-1 plan had to be modified because insiders were gaming that plan.

Bringing it all together

To summarize our chapter on insider transactions:

1. Insiders of companies include the management of the company, the members of the board of directors and 10% owners. These insiders are required to file a Form 4 with the SEC with the details of their

purchase, sale or option exercise within two business days of the transaction. Multiple studies conducted over several decades have consistently shown that insiders tend to outperform the market.

2. Insider purchases provide a stronger signal than insider sales. Given the thousands of transactions filed with the SEC each year, you have to rely on certain strategies to find attractive opportunities among the insider purchases.

3. When a group of insiders are purchasing shares of the same company at the same time, it is known as a cluster purchase. Cluster purchases indicate that multiple insiders are willing to put their own money on the line because they expect the future of the company to be bright.

4. Pay attention to industries or sectors that are in trouble and experiencing a significant amount of insider buying. When the dust settles, the strongest companies in that industry are likely to do well.

5. I like to see insider buying by the Chair of the board, especially when they are either the founder of the company or have served on the board over a multi-decade period. This is especially true for cyclical sectors like energy or mining.

6. Insider buying by independent directors who have an investment background can help you identify investment opportunities.

7. The sell/buy ratio divides aggregate insider selling in a week by aggregate insider buying in the same week. On average insiders sell 30 times as much stock as they buy. While rare, instances where aggregate insider buying exceeds aggregate insider selling can provide a bullish macro-signal.

8. Flip-floppers are insiders that were previously selling but suddenly decided to change direction and started buying instead, or vice-versa. If this happens within a six month period, the securities act of 1934 requires insiders to disgorge any profits from the trade back to the company.

9. Insiders' sales don't provide a strong signal but pay attention to companies where multiple insiders are selling stock at the same time and especially when the stock is declining.

10. Company insiders are aware that market participants are tracking their actions and sometimes buy stock just to signal the market and drum up enthusiasm for the stock. In some extreme cases, they go so far as to issuing a press release drawing attention to their purchase.

In conclusion, insider transactions can help us discover and invest in companies that can transform a portfolio and provide excellent long-term returns, as long as we can distinguish the real signal from the noise.

In the next few chapters, as we explore other event-driven strategies, you will find insider transactions making a guest appearance in several of them.

CHAPTER 4

STOCK BUYBACKS

Henry Singleton, the co-founder and CEO of Teledyne (NYSE: TDY) was described in *The Outsiders* as a master capital allocator. In the early days of Teledyne, Singleton used the company's expensive stock to acquire 130 companies over an eight-year period. I can't begin to imagine the kind of regulatory scrutiny that would receive in the modern environment.

Once good acquisitions became scarce, and Teledyne's stock was cheap, Mr. Singleton turned around and over a 12-year period bought back an astounding 90% of the company. It was not surprising that Teledyne (TDY) generated 20.4% annual returns from 1963 to 1990, compared to 11.6% for the S&P 500 during the same period.

In other words, a $1,000 invested in the S&P 500 at the start of 1963 would have turned into $21,607 by the end of 1990. The same $1,000 invested in Teledyne stock would have grown to $180,943, thanks to the wonders of compounding.

Stock buybacks

When a company buys back its own stock, it reduces the number of shares that are outstanding, thereby allowing its profits to be distributed across a smaller pool of shares. This increases earnings per share and, if the company pays a dividend, allows for payment of a larger dividend to the remaining shareholders.

The most obvious reason for buying back shares is to return value to existing shareholders, especially when the stock is cheap. But companies employ stock buybacks for other reasons, including offsetting dilution from stock options awarded to employees and reducing shares outstanding to juice reported earnings per share (EPS).

Unless their stock is held in a retirement account, shareholders must pay taxes on dividends. Buybacks allow companies to return value to shareholders in a tax-efficient manner. If a buyback is done at the right time, the value of the company should increase over time and this will translate into a higher share price. Investors are not taxed on this increase in value until they decide to sell the stock. The Inflation Reduction Act of 2022 introduced a new 1% tax on stock buybacks. This 1% tax, which went into effect in 2023 and requires the company that is buying back stock to pay the tax, is a small hurdle for companies to overcome considering the long-term benefit from buybacks.

Open-market purchases

There are two ways in which companies buy back shares. The first option is through open-market purchases. This option gives the company the most flexibility, as it allows them to spread out purchases over a period of several months or years. They can start and stop purchasing whenever they see fit. If market conditions are not favorable, the company might not follow through on a buyback even after announcing one. We will discuss this in more detail when we cover signaling by companies later in this chapter.

On the other hand, if market conditions are favorable and the company's management thinks the stock is particularly cheap, they might enter into an accelerated share repurchase (ASR) program with an investment bank. The bank helps the company rapidly execute its buyback by acquiring large blocks of shares on the company's behalf. The bank might deliver an agreed-upon number of shares to the company immediately and then deliver the rest over a short period of time.

Tender offers

The second option is known as a tender offer. Through this method, the company broadly announces to its shareholders that it is willing to buy back its stock at a certain price. The price offered is usually above the current market price, to entice existing shareholders to tender their shares. In certain instances, the company provides a range for the tender offer, and shareholders can select the price at which they are prepared to tender their shares.

For example, in their tender offer in August 2020, Herbalife Nutrition (NYSE: HLF) wanted to repurchase $750m worth of shares and was willing to pay between $44.75 per share and $50 per share. If you had owned Herbalife shares and tendered them for $45, there was a higher probability that the company would have accepted your shares compared to an investor who tendered at $50, provided the offer was oversubscribed.

Tender offers are open for a specified period and sometimes include a minimum tender condition, whereby a company only proceeds with the buyback if a certain number of shares are tendered.

If you are a shareholder and wish to sell your shares to the company, you must tender them through your broker. Once you do this, the shares get locked and cannot be traded. If the company were to accept your tendered shares, the broker would deposit cash into your account. If on the other hand not enough shares were tendered, the company might cancel the tender. Your shares would then be released, leaving you free to trade them on the open market.

There is another possible outcome, in which shareholders tender more shares than the company wants to buy. In this case your shares would be subject to proration. In other words, the shares would be accepted proportionally, with only some of the shares accepted and the rest returned to you.

Most companies these days prefer the flexibility of open-market purchases, and tender offers—besides those associated with an acquisition—have become increasingly rare. When a company is acquiring its own shares through a tender offer, it is known as an "issuer tender offer." You can find issuer tender offers on the SEC's website.[8]

Issuer tender offers are also used to repurchase bonds or preferred shares. For example, Bank of America (NYSE: BAC) announced a tender offer in November 2022 to buy back up to $1.5bn worth of certain preferred shares.[9] In each case, you would have to look through the filing to understand the specifics of the offer.

Preferred shares generally pay a higher dividend but don't participate in the upside of common stock. If the company does well and reports higher earnings over time, the common stock is likely to go up, but the preferred shares will not. They are more sensitive to what is happening to interest rates. When interest rates rise, preferred shares could see their value drop because investors have an alternative option that might pay a higher interest rate or a similar interest rate with lower risk. This is exactly what happened in 2022 when the Federal Reserve increased interest rates rapidly to combat inflation, and the value of existing preferred shares and bonds dropped. Bank of America wanted to use this opportunity to buy back preferred shares that had dropped in value and retire them through a tender offer.

In certain scenarios, tender offers provide an interesting opportunity to lock in a small but guaranteed profit.

These days you can trade a small number of shares of a specific company and even trade a fraction of one share. For example, if you wanted to invest $1,000 in Apple (Nasdaq: AAPL), you could choose to buy 6.67 shares of the company if it traded at $150 per share at the time of your purchase.

There was a time when this was not possible, and you had to buy shares in multiples of 100. These were known as round lots. Any quantities of less than 100 shares were known as odd lots.

Some tender offers (though fewer now than in the past) have an "odd lot clause," whereby if you tendered less than 100 shares the company would accept them at the tender price. This removed uncertainty about whether your shares would be accepted and guaranteed a profit if you were able to buy the stock below the tender price on the open market and then tender your shares. The limitation was that you could not do this with any more than 99 shares.

Why does this option exist in tender offers, and why has it become increasingly rare in recent years?

Companies must keep records of all their shareholders for various purposes including issuing dividends, issuing more shares in case of a stock split, issuing rights to existing shareholders to allow them to purchase additional shares, distributing shares in a spinoff, among other things.

In the days before computers simplified this process, companies could reduce their administrative burden by repurchasing stock from investors who held a small number of shares—hence the birth of the odd lot clause. Participating in odd lot tender offers used to be a near-guaranteed method of earning a profit and hence their popularity increased among investors. This increase in popularity happened at a time when companies started scaling back on including an odd lot clause. This translated into the stock price of a company announcing an odd lot tender offer moving up rapidly, making it difficult for investors to capture what was previously a near-guaranteed profit. There have also been instances where the odd lot provision was removed or modified.

A recent example of a tender offer with an odd lot provision was the offer by ADT (NYSE: ADT) to repurchase $1.2bn of its own stock at a price of $9 per share. The company had planned on acquiring 133m shares, and the tender offer was significantly oversubscribed with 732.1m shares tendered. The company accepted all odd lots in full, and after that the proration factor was 18.17%. In other words, for round lot investors, only 18.17 shares of each 100 shares they tendered were accepted.

Given the low price of this tender offer, the maximum profit for the odd lot tender offer was limited. ADT announced the tender offer on October 13, 2022, and the stock closed trading the next day at $8.01. Investors who used the regular tender offer option also did well, as 18.17% of their shares were accepted at $9 per share and the stock remained above the $8.01 level for several weeks after the tender offer, peaking at just over $10 in December 2022. This was a situation where both odd lot and regular investors who tendered shares benefited, but given the low price of the stock, the profits odd lot tender investors made were small compared to regular investors.

Management's judgment and cyclical industries

Buybacks reflect management's judgment in determining when the stock is cheap and when it is expensive. When the stock is cheap, you would expect management to buy back shares. When it is expensive, they should issue more shares through a secondary offering or use stock to acquire other companies.

Buybacks also signal that management is unable to invest in new lines of business or find attractive acquisition opportunities.

Buybacks generally get a bad rap because there are several notable instances where companies have repurchased shares at exactly the wrong time. Citigroup (NYSE: C) used precious capital to repurchase shares right before the housing-related financial crisis in 2007–2009. The company was subsequently forced to receive the biggest bailout of any American bank.

The most common buyback mistakes I observe are related to cyclical companies, and we explore two such industries to understand how cycles work and why management teams in these industries make mistakes.

Shipping

The shipping industry is notorious for being a cyclical industry. When times are good and demand is up, shipping companies that transport goods across the oceans can charge more for their services. Profits increase and these companies are flush with cash. This usually leads to some shipping companies ordering new ships to meet the increase in demand and to take advantage of high shipping rates. Unfortunately, once new ships are ordered they can take years to build and deliver.

If the newly minted ships are delivered after the economy has cooled and demand has waned, the shipping companies cannot command the same prices for transporting goods as they did when the orders for the new ships were placed. Even if the good times have continued and the economy is humming along at a fast clip, if too many shipping companies end up with new ships at around the same time, supply will exceed demand and freight rates will drop. This leads to a decline in profits and eventual losses. The bottom of the cycle is marked by bankruptcies and then consolidation among the remaining companies through mergers and acquisitions.

Stocks often look the cheapest at their cyclical peaks and companies are also flush with cash at those moments. Cyclical companies at their peaks are value traps and investors that have not experienced multiple cycles or don't understand the dynamics of a particular industry often learn costly lessons after they buy these value traps.

Companies aren't immune to this phenomenon either. They often end up buying back stock near cyclical peaks and just as the cycle is about to change course and start heading down.

Energy

The start of 2023 saw one of the largest share buyback announcements with the energy giant Chevron (NYSE: CVX) announcing a whopping $75bn buyback. The only other companies that have announced buybacks of similar magnitude are Alphabet (Nasdaq: GOOG) and Apple (Nasdaq: APPL), which announced buybacks of $70bn and $90bn respectively in April 2022.

Chevron was not the only company in the energy sector to announce share buybacks, and you could see buyback announcements galore across both large and small energy producers, oil services companies, and companies that transport oil and gas across continents through pipelines. To understand the genesis of this enthusiasm for buybacks among energy companies, we have to take a trip back in time.

In the 2010's there was a new energy revolution in the United States with a boom in hydraulic fracturing or fracking, a technology that allows energy companies to drill horizontally through rock and inject a combination of water, sand, and chemicals to release oil and gas that was previously inaccessible.

This boom in fracking increased oil and gas production significantly, helping the United States achieve energy independence. We soon went from fears of hitting "peak oil" to a big surplus in oil and especially natural gas. Unfortunately investors in these fracking companies did not benefit from this boom. The frackers consumed boatloads of capital, pumped a lot of oil out of the ground, and at the end of the day had little profit to show for it.

The reason for the surprising lack of profit was that the frackers decided not to join one of the few legal cartels in the world, OPEC. Cartels, where a group of companies conspire to fix prices in such a way that it helps their profits but hurts consumers because there is no competition between the companies, are illegal. Organization of the Petroleum Exporting Countries (OPEC) is a global cartel consisting of oil producing countries that work together to control the supply of oil and, as a result, its price.

When I think of fracking companies, the first thing that comes to mind is the hilarious "meet the frackers" presentation delivered by Greenlight Capital's noted hedge fund manager David Einhorn at the Sohn Conference in 2015.[10] I have a great deal of respect for Mr. Einhorn, and I enjoyed reading his book *Fooling Some of the People All of the Time, A Long Short Story* about his multi-year battle shorting Allied Capital.[11]

For a period of time, Mr. Einhorn was right about the frackers as they continued to consume ever-increasing amounts of capital to drill holes and flood the energy market with excess supply. Since the frackers were not aligned with OPEC in terms of constraining supply when needed to stabilize price, OPEC went on the offensive. They engineered a price war that brought the frackers to their knees, and several declared bankruptcy.

However, this has changed in recent years, with companies like Continental Resources and Diamondback Energy reigning in costs and being selective about capital expenditures (CapEx). In other words, they decided not to drill as many holes as they used to and instead took a more measured approach to increasing production. They aligned themselves with OPEC coming out of the Covid-19-related recession and the price of oil spiked, leading to massive profits for frackers and integrated oil companies like Chevron alike.

One example was the fracking company Diamondback Energy (NASDAQ: FANG) that announced a massive $2bn buyback representing nearly 14% of the company's market cap in mid-September 2021. The company explicitly stated that they were going to focus on returning value to shareholders and hold the line on production. The company went on to buy back shares after the announcement, declared a series of special dividends in the next few quarters and increased its regular dividend. The stock, which was trading close to $80 when the buyback announcement was made, went on to double and reached a peak of a little over $160 less than 10 months later.

The buyback announcements by the energy sector companies were made near a cyclical top, but the driving factors were very different from the kind of announcements we saw from Citigroup in 2006.

For every Citigroup there are also counter examples like the Teledyne example we discussed earlier. As investors, we must look past anecdotal data to what aggregate information across long cycles tells us about the effectiveness of buybacks. Keeping industry dynamics in mind will also help you understand which buybacks are from companies making a mistake near a cyclical top and which ones are from companies in a cyclical industry that are attempting to moderate supply.

Uber cannibals

Renowned value investor Mohnish Pabrai, and Yingzhuo Zhao, a quantitative analyst at Dhandho Funds, published an article in *Forbes* in December 2016 titled "Move Over Small Dogs Of The Dow, Here Come The Uber Cannibals."[12]

Heeding Charlie Munger's advice to pay attention to the cannibals, they decided to run a backtest from 1992 to 2016 building a portfolio of five companies that had repurchased the most stock in the prior year. The portfolio was rebalanced on March 18 of each year to pick up any new companies that fit their criteria.

Buybacks were not the only criterion they used. They filtered out stocks with a market cap below $100m, insurance companies, and companies that were not growing revenue, added a value criterion by picking up companies with a price/sales ratio below 2.5, and made sure that the buyback percentage over the dividend yield for the last year was greater than 2%.

I wrote the following in a blog post several years ago about their results:

> There has been a lot of academic research over the years that shows the superior performance of companies buying back their own stock. Recent research into the "uber cannibals", defined as the top five companies buying back their own shares, by Mohnish Pabrai, shows that the uber cannibals have outperformed the S&P 500 Index by 6.3% annualized over a 26-year period.

It was fascinating to see that companies like the auto parts retailer AutoZone and the home builder NVR that dominated their list since 2001 are still consistent buyers of their own stock. When Mr. Pabrai and Mr. Zhao published the article, AutoZone had bought back 80% of its shares outstanding over the last 20 years and NVR had repurchased 75%. From 2019 to 2023, AutoZone bought back an additional 25% of its shares and NVR retired more than 12% of its shares outstanding.

Another thing that stood out when reviewing their portfolio was that while some companies appeared two years in a row, AutoZone and NVR were exceptions. The companies that made it to the top five were often new companies, lending credence to the assertion that companies often mistakenly buy back stock during cyclical peaks.

In recent years, Apple (NASDAQ: AAPL) is a good example of a cannibal that has both executed well on the business front and repurchased large swaths of stock at great prices. Apple retired more than 20% of its shares outstanding between 2018 and 2022. As discussed earlier, Apple also announced a $90bn additional buyback in 2021 and 2022. Alphabet's buybacks have been more modest, with the company retiring a little more than 5% of shares outstanding between 2019 and 2022. Alphabet also announced a $70bn buyback in April 2022.

Image 4.1: Change in shares outstanding for Apple (AAPL)

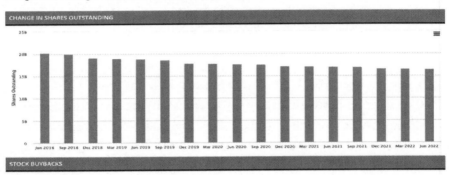

Source: InsideArbitrage.com

The company that takes the crown as the king of the cannibals over the last five years is the dialysis services provider DaVita (NYSE: DVA), which retired nearly 50% of its shares outstanding from Q3 2017 to Q3 2022. The company doubled its earnings per share over during that period, but the stock barely appreciated since most of the earnings per share growth was driven by the reduction in shares outstanding. Revenue growth was less than 20% over the period, indicating DaVita would not have made Mr. Pabrai's list of uber cannibals. Berkshire Hathaway started building a stake in DaVita in 2012–2013 and in 2022 owned about 40% of the company.

I focus on companies where the announced buyback represents a large part of their market cap and not just on companies announcing the largest buybacks in absolute dollar terms like Apple (NASDAQ: AAPL) and Alphabet (NASDAQ: GOOG). A good recent example is Franchise

Group's $500m buyback announcement, which represented more than 31% of the company's market cap at announcement on May 18, 2022.

Franchise Group (NASDAQ: FRG) is the holding company for businesses like Pet Supplies Plus, American Freight, The Vitamin Shoppe, Buddy's Home Furnishings, and Liberty Tax Service. The company's buyback is expected to occur over a three-year period. While this might appear to be an attractive opportunity, you have to look beyond a company's market cap. Franchise Group has net debt of $2.35bn on its balance sheet, bringing the company's enterprise value up to $3.92bn. Should a company that is as leveraged as Franchise Group buy back stock instead of paying down debt?

The simple answer to this question is no. A more nuanced answer would look at the cost of the debt compared to current interest rates to see if the debt is low cost and does not come due for several years. It would consider current profitability, the ability to easily pay the interest on the debt and future expected growth. It would also look at whether the stock is extremely undervalued and presents the best allocation of capital at that point in time.

Buyback announcements versus actual buybacks

Buyback announcements are sometimes not followed by actual share repurchases. It is important to understand if a company is actually buying back its stock, has announced buybacks to offset shareholder dilution from stock-based compensation, or is just trying to signal the market. This is one of the reasons it is important to track both the announcements and the actual reduction in shares outstanding. Companies are required to disclose the number of shares outstanding in their 10-Q quarterly and 10-K annual filings with the SEC.

Double-dipper buybacks and insider purchases

I developed a screen to identify interesting investment ideas, called the "Double Dipper." The Double Dipper sounds like the name of a roller coaster at Six Flags (NYSE: SIX) but it is a list of companies that are buying back their shares while their insiders are independently buying stock on the open market for their own portfolios.

The screen provides a double signal, showing where the actions of insiders align with those of the board of directors—the group that decides if a company should buy back its stock or not.

Case study 1: Avis Budget Group

Joe Ferraro happened to take on the role of interim CEO at the car rental company Avis Budget Group (NASDAQ: CAR) at one of the most difficult times in the company's history. After serving as president, Americas where his responsibilities included the brands Avis, Budget, Payless and Zipcar across North America, South America and the Caribbean, he went on to take the top job at the start of 2020, culminating nearly 40 years of experience with the company.

At the same time, Bernardo Hees was appointed independent chairman of the board in February 2020. Mr. Hees, a Brazilian economist and businessman, had previously served as the CEO of Burger King and The Kraft Heinz Company. He was a partner at 3G Capital, a global private equity firm with Brazilian roots. The firm had partnered with Warren Buffett in 2013 to acquire Heinz and later merged it with Kraft in 2015 to create The Kraft Heinz Company. Mr. Hees' experience with reducing costs at both Burger King and then Kraft Heinz would prove invaluable to Avid Budget.

The same month Mr. Hees joined the board as chairman, the floor dropped out from under the company on account of global pandemic-related lockdowns and a very sharp decline in travel. Avis Budget's stock dropped from over $50 per share in February 2020 to around $7.78 in less than a month. The company, which had been planning on increasing revenue by 15% in 2020, saw more than two-thirds of its sales wiped out in the second quarter of 2020 and reported a huge loss of $6.91 per share.

The company acted very quickly to cancel its new car orders for the rest of 2020 and sold 35,000 cars from its fleet in March 2020. In the second quarter, the company disposed of an additional 100,000 cars, significantly reduced its workforce, cut back executive compensation, and removed almost $1bn of annual costs. The company negotiated rents with airports, renegotiated some of its debt covenants, and issued new debt to give it breathing room. While Avis Budget was making all these moves, its largest competitor, Hertz, ended up declaring bankruptcy.

By mid-2020 the company was on firmer footing, and Avis Budget dropped the interim part of Mr. Ferraro's title and made him CEO. Mr. Hees also became the executive chairman. The stock was already recovering rapidly and, just one year later, the company reported a profit of $5.63 per share in the second quarter of 2021 compared to that record loss in Q2 2020.

The pandemic-fueled stimulus bubble pushed the stock to peak close to $300 in November 2021 before coming down to earth. Despite the extreme volatility, the stock is still up more than 260% from its pre-pandemic peak in February 2020 and up 1,549% as I write this almost three years after the March 2020 low.

What were some of the factors that helped Avis Budget to not just survive but thrive? Competent management that was driven to quick action in the early stages of the pandemic helped. So did the troubles at Hertz, which was planning on selling 180,000 cars from its fleet of over half a million cars as part of its bankruptcy process. Supply chain issues constrained the supply of new cars. Once lockdowns ended and travel demand came back strong, there were fewer cars left for consumers to rent, and rental prices spiked sharply across the board.

Over a two-year period in 2021 and 2022, Avis Budget Group retired nearly a third of its shares outstanding through buybacks. The company's diluted shares outstanding dropped from 70.5m at the end of 2020 to 48.4m by the end of 2022.

While this in itself is not an astounding feat, by the time the company filed its 2022 10-K report with the SEC on February 16, 2023, it reported that as of February 10, 2023, shares outstanding had dropped to 39.47m, pointing to a significant acceleration in its buyback activity in early 2023.

During this time, the company's executive chairman, Bernardo Hees, purchased nearly $15m worth of shares across three insider transactions.

The company had been a big buyer of its own stock even before the pandemic. What was absolutely fascinating about the company's approach to buybacks was that they didn't stop making them during Q1 2020. Based on the average price of $22.49 the company paid during Q1 2020 they continued buying during the worst of the March 2020 decline, when the world was essentially coming to a stop and travel had all but frozen.[13]

For the next four quarters the company took a breather before resuming buyback activity in the second quarter of 2021. The company expanded its share repurchase authorization by $325m in June 2021 and then by an additional $1bn in February 2023.

Avis Budget Group is an outstanding example of a management team that are both good operators and capital allocators, stepping up their buybacks at the right time to return value to shareholders. They also purchased shares for their own accounts multiple times in 2021 and 2022, putting the stock on my radar through the Double Dipper screen.

Signaling through buybacks

When large stock buybacks are announced by companies, investors tend to bid up the shares. Both insider buying and buyback announcements result in a short-term upward movement in the stock that is well documented in long-term studies, and company managements are often aware of this phenomenon.

Just like insider purchases, it sometimes feels like companies are attempting to signal the market or are genuinely misguided in their assumption that their stock is undervalued when they announce massive buybacks.

According to a 1995 academic study by Dr. David Ikenberry et al., companies that buy back stock beat the stock price performance of their peers by 12.1% over a four-year period from the date of initial announcement.[14] While the study looked at buybacks from 1980 to 1990, recent studies and analysis such as the one described in the uber cannibals section of this chapter continue to point to outperformance by these firms. One of the things from the 1995 paper that stood out was that the performance of value stocks was a stunning average abnormal return of 45.3%. For "glamor" stock—what we could call growth stocks these days—no abnormal returns were observed.

How do we as investors go about avoiding the companies that are announcing buybacks:

1. for the initial positive reaction from the market,

2. to meet certain metrics like an improved earnings per share number where their bonus or stock grants depend on those metrics,

3. to repurchase shares to offset stock dilution from employee options,

4. where they are mistaken about the valuation of the company?

Deliberate signaling

Let's first consider companies that are deliberately engaging in signaling. Dr. Ikenberry co-authored another paper 15 years after the one recently discussed, titled "Share Repurchases as a Potential Tool to Mislead Investors" that looked at how companies and their management teams used buyback announcements to influence investor sentiment.[15]

The researchers examined 7,628 open market purchases announced in the U.S. over a 20-year period from 1980 to 2000 and found that while firms that were attempting to convey a false signal to the market saw the same positive performance in the short term as other companies, in the long term they did not enjoy the same outperformance.

The firms engaging in this conduct had management teams that were under a lot of pressure to boost their share price and were incentivized to engage in this activity because their compensation had a lot of exposure to stock options.

These kinds of companies had declining sales, were experiencing a sharp decline in their stock price, and analysts were revising their earnings estimates downward. These indicators give investors enough information to figure out which companies might be engaging in signaling and which ones truly believe their stock is undervalued.

The one bright spot from the researchers' analysis was that the proportion of companies they suspected of engaging in these practices was well below 10% of the companies they analyzed.

Misguided valuations

Now that we have a better understanding of how we can spot companies that are engaging in signaling, what about those that are genuinely misguided in their belief that their stock is undervalued?

We have a trio of professors from Boston College to help us answer this question. In their fascinating paper titled "Do Managers Always Know Better? The Relative Accuracy of Management and Analyst Forecasts" Amy Hutton, Lian Fen Lee and Susan Shu found that analysts have a forecasting advantage over company management when macroeconomic factors like the business cycle, commodity prices, and the regulatory environment had a large impact on the company. [16] This suggests it can be beneficial to factor in analyst forecasts when assessing a company's motives for issuing buybacks.

I had come to the same conclusion from observing insider transactions across hundreds of companies for well over a decade, and it was encouraging to see that an academic study formally confirmed my hypothesis.

Conversely, the research team found that for companies that are experiencing some sort of internal issue such as high inventory growth, and for companies that house multiple business divisions or have an opaque business model (I call these companies "black boxes"), management teams have an edge over analysts.

When assessing buybacks these types of companies are best avoided unless you have some special insight and can spend a lot of time understanding the various components of the company, or at least the parts that are visible to the general public. It is not surprising that management has an edge over analysts in these kinds of companies.

One approach that can work for investors is to identify companies that are buying back stock, or whose insiders are buying back stock, when at the same time analysts are revising their earnings estimates upwards. This indicates an alignment in management and analyst expectations and potentially a good investment opportunity.

I use both insider buying and stock buybacks as idea generation mechanisms and not as the primary signal for addition to my portfolio.

There is no substitute for doing further research to understand companies and their valuations before investing your hard-earned money in them.

Case study 2: Bed, Bath & Beyond

Retail is a particularly challenging business, with low margins, fickle consumer tastes, and a large number of moving parts. I recollect buying my first music system from a department store chain called Montgomery Ward just months before it closed its doors forever. Over the years I have watched a string of retailers declare bankruptcy including Sears, RadioShack, Mervyn's, Toys "R" Us, Gymboree, Mattress Firm, American Apparel, Aeropostale, Payless, Vitamin World and more.

What is remarkable about this short list is that it includes various sub-sectors of retail ranging from electronics to children's toys. Another company that is likely to join their ranks at the time of writing is Bed, Bath & Beyond (NASDAQ: BBBY). The home of the "20% off coupon" to buy bed sheets, towels and more is now a penny stock and is widely expected to go bankrupt.

I had attempted shopping at Bed, Bath & Beyond a few times and, more often than not, walked out without wanting to buy anything at the store. It wasn't exactly the price, or the vast number of options provided, but something always felt off about the stores. Bed, Bath & Beyond did not have the price leadership of Costco, the convenience of Target (NYSE: TGT), the treasure hunt characteristics of The TJX Companies (NYSE: TJX), or the air of exclusivity of the company formerly known as Restoration Hardware (NYSE: RH). The company was in sore need of outstanding merchandising and a way to break out of its mold as the forgotten middle child of retail big box stores in nondescript suburban strip malls.

Towards that end the company hired Mark Tritton as CEO in November 2019, just two months before the appointment of Joe Ferraro at Avis

Budget Group, as discussed in our earlier case study. Unlike Avis Budget Group, which picked a 40-year veteran of the company, Bed, Bath & Beyond went looking outside and picked Target's chief merchandising officer to take the top job. Less than six months later, the company appointed Gustavo Arnal CFO in May 2020. Mr. Arnal had previously served as the CFO of Avon.

Another commonality between Bed, Bath & Beyond and companies like Aeropostale is the amount of money they destroyed through badly timed stock buybacks. Between October 2020 and March 2022 Bed, Bath & Beyond burned through almost $1bn worth of capital through share buybacks. Not only did the company use up precious reserves during challenging market conditions, it accelerated part of its buyback program and completed it in one year instead of three.

Image 4.2: Bed, Bath & Beyond buybacks

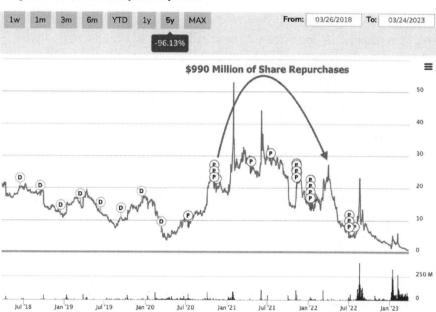

Source: InsideArbitrage.com

During the Covid-19 pandemic a large number of individual or retail investors started trading stocks and exchanging ideas on message boards like Reddit. They would exchange information about stocks through images with funny captions, also referred to as memes. One group of stocks that were particularly attractive to these traders were beaten-down companies with a large short interest. These companies were often ones with declining sales or a large amount of debt that the short sellers figured would drop in price or eventually go bankrupt. As described in our chapter on merger arbitrage, short sellers initially sell shares they don't have by borrowing them from a broker and plan to eventually buy them back at a lower price to return the borrowed stock to the broker. In other words, they sell high and buy low if all goes according to plan. If, on the other hand, the price of the stock rises, the short sellers end up with a loss and at some point are forced to cover their position by buying back the stock and closing their short position. To calculate the short interest, you divide the number of shares short by the average daily volume traded. For example, if there are 10m shares short and the average daily volume of shares traded is 1m then the short interest is 10. In other words, it would take short sellers approximately 10 days to cover their position assuming all buying is done by the short sellers. Several websites including the Nasdaq website report on short interest at periodic intervals.

Companies like Bed, Bath & Beyond, Gamestop and AMC Entertainment became meme stock favorites and a large number of retail traders started buying them, causing the share price to spike rapidly. This forced investors that were short the stock to cover their positions by buying at these elevated prices. Buying begets more buying and companies like Gamestop saw their stock prices shoot up rapidly ("to the moon" as the meme stock crowd used to say) before coming back to earth. Gamestop saw its stock price rise from under $8 in September 2020 to a high of $325 by January 2021. Similarly Bed, Bath & Beyond saw its stock price spike from under $12 in September 2020 to over $35 by January 2021.

As you can see from Image 4.2, most of the buybacks at Bed, Bath & Beyond happened when the stock became a meme favorite and was trading at elevated prices. For years before that, the stock was range-bound, oscillating between $10 and $20 per share.

Bed, Bath & Beyond's balance sheet, which had $1.4bn in cash and $1.5bn in debt in February 2020, was decimated by this misguided capital allocation policy and a string of losses that exceed over $1bn. By August 2022, the balance sheet was left with just $135m in cash compared to $1.7bn in debt.

The tragedy was not just limited to the company's financial statements or the fact that it was now closing stores and laying off employees. Bed, Bath & Beyond's CFO, Gustavo Arnal, plunged to his death from New York's Tribeca skyscraper in what was ruled a suicide. Both Mr. Arnal and the company had been sued for participating in a pump and dump scheme during the meme stock rally of 2020 and 2021.

A combination of declining sales, losses, and a misguided capital allocation policy with buybacks at exactly the wrong time caused the company to let go of Mr. Tritton in June 2022. Less than three months later Mr. Arnal lost his life.

The two case studies covered in this chapter stand in stark contrast to each other. Both companies appointed new CEOs at around the same time, both were customer-facing businesses, both took very different approaches to how they operated during a very difficult environment, and, most importantly, their capital allocation policy using buybacks.

When looking at buyback announcements or actual buyback information, you should assess management's prior track record of capital allocation decisions. When did they choose to issue debt or pay down debt? Did their prior M&A activity spur growth in both revenue and improve net margin? Did they issue or buy back stock when it was expensive or cheap respectively in the past? Beyond this assessment, you should also look at the company qualitatively to understand how it is positioned in relation to peers in its industry, the intrinsic value of the company compared to its current market price and any macroeconomic factors that are either favorable or create headwinds for the company. Finally check to see if the management team is buying stock on the open market with their own money or selling stock even as the company is buying back stock.

The dark side of buybacks

In his September 2014 *Harvard Business Review* paper "Profits Without Prosperity," author William Lazonick takes an alternative view of buybacks.[17] Dr. Lazonick is professor emeritus of economics at University of Massachusetts, Lowell. The paper discussed the negative side of buybacks and is in stark contrast to the rosy picture painted in the Pabrai article.

Dr. Lazonick states that allocation of profits to share buybacks leaves very little for companies to invest in productive capabilities or higher income for employees. This is true in many cases where firms use the cash generated to fund repurchases instead of using it for R&D or acquisitions.

While I have some sympathy for the author's claims, his suggestion that buybacks should be entirely banned is a little extreme. The 1% buyback tax that came into effect in 2023 appears to be headed in the direction the author would like the government to go, though I consider this tax unnecessary and hope it does not increase in the future.

2022 was a challenging year for the markets as multiple bubbles unraveled simultaneously. This did not stop companies from announcing over $1 trillion in buybacks that year. The largest uber cannibals delivered bad results in a challenging market, lending some credence to the criticism buybacks receive from authors like Mr. Lazonick as well as the general press.

These results did not stop companies from announcing over $100bn worth of buybacks in January 2023, with just three companies including Chevron (NYSE: CVX), BlackRock (NYSE: BLK) and Costco accounting for $84bn of those announcements.

Buybacks, when done prudently, can be excellent capital allocation tools in the hands of skilled management teams and a signal to investors to pay attention to those companies.

Bringing it all together

To summarize our chapter on stock buybacks:

1. A company that issues new shares when its stock is expensive and buys them back when it is cheap creates a lot of shareholder value over time.

2. Companies can buy back their stock through open-market purchases, through an accelerated share repurchase agreement with an investment bank or through a tender offer. Some tender offers include an odd-lot provision where the tendered shares are accepted if an investor is tendering 99 shares or less.

3. Companies buy back their stock because they believe the stock is inexpensive and the market is not recognizing its true value. In some cases this belief can be misguided. Management teams of companies in a cyclical industry end up buying near the peak of the cycle because the stock appears cheap and the company is usually flush with cash.

4. In some instances companies also buy back their stock to offset dilution from stock-based compensation, to juice earnings-per-share numbers or to signal the market. Investors have to do qualitative work to understand the motivations behind the buyback.

5. Identifying companies where insiders are buying shares on the open market with their own money while the company is buying back its own stock can help surface investments worthy of further research.

6. Uber cannibals are companies that repurchased the most stock in the prior year. These are growing companies that trade at a price/sales ratio below 2.5 and repurchased 2% more stock than their dividend yield. These companies outperformed the S&P 500 Index by 6.3% annualized over a 26-year study period.

CHAPTER 5

SPACS

IN THE FIRST chapter of this book I recounted my first experience with a blank check company, where two entrepreneurs raised money from investors first and then went looking for a company to acquire. You may remember that they eventually landed in Eugene, Oregon, where they acquired a jewelry company called Jody Coyote. The duo rapidly grew the company, expanding from 1,200 stores that carried their jewelry to nearly 4,000 in their first 18 months.

Special Purpose Acquisition Companies (SPACs) are set up to raise money through an IPO with the intention of acquiring an existing company, though at the outset they don't know which company that will be. The pool of money raised could be private or public as it is with most SPACs. The process of forming a SPAC provides a faster and simpler way for the operating business to go public without having to go through a long, expensive IPO process. Unfortunately, the simplicity and ease of going public without a lot of scrutiny also leads to problems, which we will get into later.

Hunt for an operating company (time is of the essence)

Investors who are involved in a SPAC IPO, or who buy it on the open market after it starts trading, get "units" of the SPAC, usually priced at $10 a pop. The units usually include shares and warrants, though in a few select cases such as the SPAC Khosla Ventures Acquisition Co. II (that went on to acquire the social networking company Nextdoor (NYSE: KIND)), no warrants are included. The units split into common shares and warrants 52 days after the IPO. After the split both common shares and warrants start trading independently.

Warrants allow you to buy common shares at a predetermined price in the future and usually expire several years later. Call options are derivative instruments that in some ways are similar to warrants. Call options allow you to buy a stock at a specific price for a certain period of time, usually a few weeks or months. Call options that expire more than a year later are called "long-term equity anticipation securities" (LEAPs).

For example, if you think General Electric (NYSE: GE) is going to do well under CEO Larry Culp's leadership, but it is going to take him a few years to turn around the lumbering giant, you could buy $100 LEAP call options that expire three years later. If the stock is below $100, you don't exercise the option because you can buy it cheaper on the stock market and lose the premium paid for the option. If you paid a premium of $15 for the option, the position would generate a profit once the stock goes up over $115 ($100 strike price and $15 for the premium), not taking trading costs into account. While LEAPs give you a lot of time to get your thesis right and see if Mr. Culp can recreate the magic he performed at his previous company, Danaher (NYSE: DHR), most LEAPs only let you go out to an expiration date 39 months in the future. As I write this, I am only able to find GE LEAPs that go out 21 months. You will also pay a significant premium to have the option without incurring the obligation to purchase the stock.

In contrast, warrants can have a longer duration and can expire in five, 10 or even 15 years.

After a business combination with an operating company is announced, investors can either vote for the transaction or redeem their shares for roughly the IPO price of $10 per share plus a little extra. The little extra comes from interest earned on the money raised from the IPO while the SPAC was looking for a company to acquire. The warrants continue to remain outstanding. The lockup period during which insiders are prohibited from selling stock is usually longer, at 12 months compared to six months for a traditional IPO.

The structure of a SPAC does not allow sponsors to extract management fees or other kinds of fees from the capital raised in the IPO, hence IPO investors are likely to get back the $10 per unit they invested plus a little more. If a SPAC sponsor like Chamath Palihapitiya's Social Capital does not find an operating business within a specified period of time (usually 12 to 24 months) they have to return the IPO proceeds to investors.

SPAC arbitrage and upside from warrants

The real opportunity in this strategy comes from the optionality the warrants provide and any increase in the price of the common shares after an attractive business combination is announced. You can purchase SPAC units right after the IPO and before they split into shares and warrants. If you don't like the business the SPAC decides to acquire or want to reduce your downside risk, you can tender the shares during the business combination vote. You get the $10 you paid for the SPAC (plus a little interest) and get to keep the warrants for free.

If the post-merger company—often referred to as a de-SPAC—is successful, the warrants could be worth a lot of money in the future. You can exercise the warrants and exchange them for shares in the operating company or just sell the warrants at a higher price on the open market.

The SPAC sponsors also get a lot of upside, because they typically own 20% of the combined company after the merger with an operating business.

Examples of perceived "attractive" business combinations that caused an initial share price spike include the acquisitions of Lucid Group (NASDAQ: LCID), SoFi Technologies (NASDAQ: SOFI) and Virgin Galactic (NYSE: SPCE).

What was previously a sleepy corner of capital markets kicked into high gear in 2020, with 242 SPAC IPOs compared to 26 in 2019 and 44 in 2018.

2021 was another huge year for SPACs, and both the number of SPAC IPOs as well as the amount they raised more than doubled. We went from 242 SPAC IPOs that raised $66.8bn in 2020 to 546 SPACs that raised $128bn in 2021. However, 2021 was also the year the SPAC bubble imploded, and the SEC started taking a closer look at some of the wild projections that were in the investor presentations for SPAC combinations.

Image 5.1: Number of SPACs and IPO size

Year	Number of SPACS	Total IPO Size (M)
⊞ 2019	26	$5,286
⊞ 2020	242	$66,800
⊞ 2021	546	$128,162
Grand Total	814	$200,249

Source: InsideArbitrage.com

The SPAC boom reminded me of the Chinese reverse merger group that provided great opportunities on the short side in the early part of the 2010s. Short-selling firms like Muddy Waters burnished their reputation by identifying accounting and fraud at certain companies that had gone public through a backdoor shortcut. They found public companies in the U.S. and Canada that did not have a viable business model, were trading as penny stocks and were essentially left for dead. Private Chinese companies would then merge into one of these shell public companies in a process knows as a reverse merger, and viola, they are now a publicly listed company on the NYSE, Nasdaq or other exchanges with a veneer of respectability.

Later in this chapter we will cover the performance of de-SPAC companies in more detail, but suffice to say that most of these companies performed poorly after the business combination was completed. This creates another opportunity for investors to sell short the post-merger company.

Short selling is a difficult activity under normal conditions, and one has to only read David Einhorn's *Fooling Some of the People All of the Time: A Long Short Story* to understand how challenging an endeavor it can be. Recent years have been even more difficult for short sellers as momentum and meme stocks like AMC and GameStop have obliterated the few short sellers that were still left standing. The reason legendary short seller Jim Chanos is still in the game is because his firm Kynikos Associates runs portfolios that can be 190% long and 90% short for net 100% long exposure.

Shorting low volume SPACs could prove challenging if a large number of their shares are already sold short. The borrowing fee you have to pay to short stocks could also be significant in some cases and could erode gains made from shorting the stock. The rubber hits the road when these companies have to report earnings, and in some cases they have altogether gotten rid of their earlier rosy projections.

Case study 1: WeWork

SPACs provided a public shell to certain operating companies that did not want to, or in some cases could not, go public through a regular IPO.

The IPO process includes filing a form called the S-1 with the SEC, going on a road show to meet prospective investors, working with investment bankers to determine how to price the IPO, etc.

The S-1 filing is a very detailed form that can sometimes run to hundreds of pages and has a significant amount of information about the company's business, its financial statements, the risks it could face, and why the company wants to raise money through an IPO. Oddly enough the price of the IPO might not make its way into the original filing, and there are often several rounds of amendments before it is finalized.

WeWork calls itself a "flexible space provider," and the company essentially leases out shared office spaces for various companies and businesses to use. Customers have the option of purchasing a dedicated desk in a shared office space, a private office for one to five people, an office suite for up to 20 people, or an entire private floor in one of the WeWork buildings. WeWork's memberships are either a month-by-month subscription or a pay as needed service, and the company also offers an "All-Access" pass, in which customers can access any WeWork office in the world for a higher fee.

WeWork first attempted to go public in 2019 to give its early investors and employees liquidity and potentially tap the public markets for more money to fund its money incinerating operations. After initially filing confidentially with the SEC, the S-1 WeWork filed in April 2019 was 220 pages long. Many of those pages were confusingly dedicated to pretty images of ecstatic people, a guy wearing bright yellow boxing gloves and someone scuba diving. The filing also included dozens of pages of financial statements, both audited and unaudited, and related notes.

In keeping with its innovative streak, WeWork introduced the finance world to a new phrase: "community-adjusted EBITDA." The company's charismatic and ambitious founder, Adam Neumann, and his wife, Rebekah, coined this phrase while working on the S-1 filing, which they decided to file without the help of investment bankers. The company reported a loss of $1.9bn on revenue of $1.8bn in 2018.

Earnings before interest, taxation, depreciation and amortization (EBITDA) is a mouthful but a useful metric for some investors, such as private equity firms, that want to look at the company's earnings after excluding non-cash expenses (like depreciation and amortization) as well as the impact of things like interest and taxation. These firms generally tend to load the companies they acquire with debt, and this can significantly change the interest and tax expenses post-acquisition.

Oddly enough, EBITDA has become a key metric most investors have adopted, and you hear more about EBITDA instead of free cash flow, which is what an owner of a business should be more concerned with. There is no getting away from paying interest on debt or taxes on profits.

Warren Buffett refers to free cash flow as owner's earnings. Think of it as the cash that ends up in the bank after paying all expenses of the business and any money you need to reinvest in the business to manage current operations or future growth. To provide an example of how free cash flow differs from net income, consider a company that needs to build a fancy new office tower to house its rapidly growing roster of employees. If the $400m building is built in a single year in 2022, the impact on free cash flow is felt in the same year as $400m heads out of the company's bank account in 2022. However, when the company reports its earnings, the net income is not impacted by $400m. Assuming the useful life of the office tower is 40 years, the company will spread out the expense over 40 years and register an expense of $10m a year. This $10m annual expense is called depreciation. Clearly this creates a huge divergence between net income and free cash flow in 2022. The following year, the divergence will still exist, but it will not be quite as dramatic as it was in 2022.

Divergence between net income and free cash flow is normal, but if you start seeing a pattern in which year after year free cash flow is consistently and significantly below net income, it might be a good idea to dig deeper to understand what is driving that divergence.

To give misguided investors who focus on EBITDA a helping hand, company management teams then started talking about "adjusted" EBITDA where certain items, deemed one-time expenses, were excluded from the calculation. The reasoning was that this would allow investors to more accurately compare results from one period to another, say the fourth quarter of 2023 with the fourth quarter of 2022. If the company was hit with one-time charges like a large settlement for a lawsuit in the fourth quarter of 2023 or a special tax assessment, then it could make results for that quarter look very weak compared to the same period in the prior year. Hence the adjustment to allow for an "apples-to-apples" comparison.

Unfortunately this well-intentioned adjustment philosophy became a cookie jar that some management teams used to exclude all kinds of expenses, so their results looked much better than they actually were. One-time charges kept recurring like clockwork and kept getting excluded.

What the Neumanns did with their "community-adjusted EBITDA" magic was to exclude even more expenses, such as development and design costs for their wonderfully appointed offices, marketing costs, and other basic expenses, to come up with positive earnings instead of the huge loss that a generally accepted accounting principles (GAAP) income statement would have shown. GAAP is a set of standardized accounting principles followed in the United States. Companies are required to provide an explanation of how their adjusted non-GAAP numbers reconcile with GAAP numbers, and these notes can be quite useful. This reconciliation is provided in the footnotes or notes that follow the consolidated financial statements in a company's quarterly (10-Q) or annual report (10-K) filed with the SEC.

Once investors got a chance to look behind the curtain of WeWork, the financial media and Twitter's "fintwit" community were abuzz with the absolutely shocking details, including the fact that the company had paid its founder nearly $6m worth of stock to acquire the trademark "We" from him. This triggered everything from books like *The Cult of We* to TV series such as *WeCrashed* on Apple TV+.

WeWork had to scuttle its plans to go public, and Adam Neumann ended up leaving. The company's parting gift to Neumann was a gargantuan exit package consisting of $245m worth of company stock and $200m in cash.

Almost two years later, in the midst of the SPAC bubble, the company tried its luck at going public again by merging into the SPAC BowX Acquisition Corp. BowX unitholders received one share of common stock and one-third of a warrant for each unit they held. The warrant allowed unitholders to buy shares of common stock at a price of $11.50. Keep in mind that at the time of BowX's IPO in August 2020, investors had no idea that BowX would pick WeWork as the operating company it would combine with.

Following the business combination in October 2021, the common shares started trading under the symbol WE and the warrants as WE.WT. The stock saw some initial enthusiasm, trading over $14 per share intraday within its first trading week.

In February 2022 I met with a couple of successful serial entrepreneurs at the Salesforce tower in San Francisco. The location was a WeWork office spanning the 36th, 37th and 38th floors of the tallest building in San Francisco. The views of the Bay Bridge were absolutely stunning. It is no wonder that WeWork calls it a "one-of-a-kind" location in its portfolio.

The subscription these entrepreneurs were paying to use this space was modest. Another friend who works predominantly from WeWork locations across the U.S. is also a big fan and prompted me to take a closer look at the company.

Shortly after that Salesforce Tower meeting, I did just that. I wanted to like WeWork based on the value-added product it offered and the potential for growth in both its core business and ancillary services. Occupancy of its available space was at just 59%, leaving a lot of room for growth there, and the company probably had pricing power given how inexpensive its offerings were. WeWork also offered services like Workplace by WeWork, which is space management software that other companies can use to optimize their office space.

A quick glance at WeWork's income statement and balance sheet dashed all hope of a potential turnaround story. Once valued at $50bn, the company had fallen sharply and was trading at a market cap of $4.42bn when I looked at it in February 2022. The market cap is just one part of a company's story, and once you account for net debt of $3bn on the balance sheet, WeWork's enterprise value was $7.42bn. Capitalized leases—through which the company had committed to lease space from various buildings for multiple years—of $18.4bn pushed the enterprise value up to $25.82bn.

Net debt of $3bn could be manageable for a company that generated revenue of $661m in a single quarter. Unfortunately not only was revenue shrinking, the company reported a net loss of $844m for the third quarter of 2021.

Turnaround situations rarely turn around and if they happen to be leveraged companies, the probability goes down even more. Add a money-loss operation that is seeing increasing cash outflows combined with shrinking revenue and you have a potential disaster.

WeWork's new CEO was Sandeep Mathrani, the former CEO of General Growth Properties. GGP Inc. was a real estate and shopping mall company that had just undergone a Chapter 11 bankruptcy when Mr. Mathrani took over in 2010. Mr. Mathrani was able to transform that company, eventually selling it to Brookfield Property Partners in 2018.

I figured the new CEO would use the same playbook with WeWork, wiping out equity shareholders in a bankruptcy and renegotiating both the debt and capital leases. I wrote about the company in the March 2022 Special Situations Newsletter as a short opportunity when the stock was trading at $6.40. I eventually covered the position in the model portfolio on October 30, 2022, at $2.76. As I write this in March 2023, the stock has just dipped into penny stock territory, closing at $0.97, and the market cap has shrunk to just $713m.

The performance of WeWork after the merger with a SPAC was not an anomaly but in fact is par for the course. Later in this chapter we will discuss how SPACs as a group offer fertile hunting grounds for opportunities on the short side.

Case study 2: Bowlero

Tom Shannon launched his bowling empire from humble beginnings in 1997 with the purchase of one bowling alley in Union Square in New York for $3,000 in cash and $2m of borrowed money. He transformed the bowling alley by making it a nightlife destination and turned around the bottom line, which went from losing $1m to becoming the highest-grossing bowling alley in the world. The company he founded now owns over 320 bowling alleys across the United States and grew by acquiring one of its biggest competitors, AMF Bowling Centers, in 2013, rescuing AMF from bankruptcy.

The company is now called Bowlero (NYSE: BOWL) and is the largest operator of bowling centers in the world. There are over 3,500 independently owned bowling centers in the United States, which provide opportunities for Bowlero to expand its footprint through acquisitions but also risk in that the company might take on too much debt as it pursues a growth by acquisition rollup strategy.

Companies that decide to fuel their growth through a series of acquisitions are referred to as rollups. They tend to conduct this activity in fragmented markets that have a lot of small companies or individual owners. The New York University Health System on the East Coast and Stanford Medicine on the West Coast used a similar approach by buying a bunch of community clinics in their areas. Rollups like Canada's Valeant Pharmaceuticals, and more recently Lifestance Health Group (NASDAQ: LFST), have seen their debt-burdened balance sheets weigh down the stock. Valeant Pharmaceuticals was accused of fraud, was the subject of criminal investigations, and eventually transformed itself under a new CEO, renaming itself Bausch Health Companies (NYSE: BHC) and spinning off divisions like its eye care company Bausch + Lomb (NYSE: BLCO). Rollups that take on a lot of debt to fuel growth have left a bad taste in the mouths of investors.

Getting back to Bowlero, the company chose to go public by merging with a SPAC called Isos Acquisition Corp towards the end of 2021. The stock of Isos barely budged after the business combination was announced in mid-2021, but shortly after the merger was consummated the stock started dropping from around $10 to a little over $7 by early February 2022. The stock has since more than doubled and is up more than 50% from the time it completed its business combination with Isos, despite very challenging market conditions.

Why was Bowlero's journey as a public company so different from that of WeWork? There are several reasons, both company-specific and related to the macroenvironment. Companies in 2021 and 2022 were still allowing their employees to work from home. This translated to less need for office space or WeWork rentals. The office rental environment was not quite as strong as it was pre-pandemic and we could see this in the steep decline in office REIT stocks. In contrast, consumers went back to traveling and in-person activities in earnest from mid-2021 through all of 2022. High-touch activities like bowling that were avoided during the pandemic became the norm once again.

One weekend in December 2022, when our plans to go rock climbing at an indoor facility fell through, my family and I ended up at a Bowlero facility in San Jose, California. I could see why the company was successful. The alley was modern and clean. While we ended up paying more than we usually do at our local bowling alley, the price difference was not significant enough to turn us off using Bowlero again but was enough to allow the company to turn a profit from its large bowling centers.

Favorable macro tailwinds aside, the company was growing its revenue rapidly during the three years before the Covid-19 pandemic hit and was free cash flow positive when it went public in mid-2021. Some of the resurgence in revenue seen in 2022 is likely to settle down, but the management team appears to be focused on both operations and capital allocation. The company redeemed all its outstanding warrants for $0.10 per warrant just four months after going public. Warrant holders did have a short period of time to exercise their warrants and convert them into common stock at $11.50 per share in April 2022. SPAC investors that received the warrants for free when their SPAC units split into common stock and warrants made money but did not get to enjoy the full impact of the Bowlero stock upside in 2022 unless they exercised their warrants.

The upside provided by warrants is the primary attraction for SPAC investors, but it is important to understand the operating company the SPAC is merging with to make sure that it is a viable business and not a money-losing entity or a science project with pipe dreams of future success.

The dark side of SPACS

In early 2022, I decided to download the list of all completed business combinations to see how they had performed after they had merged with an operating company. I suspected that, given the bubble in various asset classes and a dwindling supply of high-quality private business to acquire, the post-merger performance was probably not good. I was stunned by the results.

Performance was significantly worse than I expected. The group of 159 post-merger SPACs I looked at collectively lost more than 36% of their share value and only 12 out of the 159 had positive returns. And this was before the big drop in the markets in 2022.

Ross Greenspan wrote a paper on SPACs titled "Money for Nothing, Shares for Free: A Brief History of the SPAC" and some of the research he referenced in his paper really grabbed my attention.[18] The paper found that "the average four-year buy-and-hold return for second-generation SPACs was a grim negative 51.9%."

On the positive side, "one study of the third-generation SPACs found the post-IPO to the end of the pre-merger period provided an average annualized return of 9.3%."

In a market where true alpha is hard to come by, SPACs provide for fertile hunting grounds. This is one of the reasons I track both SPAC IPOs and business combinations and look for short opportunities from the universe of SPAC business combinations.

I decided to check the performance of SPACs once again in March 2023 to see what kind of impact a nearly 15-month bear market had on this group of companies.

Out of the 315 business combinations I analyzed, only 25 (8%) of them posted positive returns. The vast majority showed losses. The average performance of the full group was a loss of almost 65% and the median performance was a loss of 78%.

This kind of performance, the waning interest in SPACs, and company-specific issues sometimes cause operating companies and SPACs to call off their mergers. In those cases the SPAC would return money back to its shareholders, provided it decides not to pursue another acquisition.

Out of the 525 SPAC business combinations currently tracked on InsideArbitrage, 48 were terminated. In other words a little more than 9% of the deals fell through, which is higher than the deal failure rate of merger arbitrage situations.

As we look towards the future, I expect SPAC business combination volumes to continue declining, and the ones that actually go through are likely to be more viable businesses. This is due to both the increased scrutiny by the SEC and, more importantly, investor apathy towards companies that were nothing more than a figment of someone's imagination presented on pretty slides. I plan to continue tracking this group of companies for ideas that, much like WeWork, might turn into great short opportunities.

Bringing it all together

To summarize our chapter on SPACs:

1. SPACs or blank check companies allow an individual or group to raise money with the intention of finding an operating company that they can merge with in the future. In the words of Venture Capitalist Don Butler, "You can think of it like: an IPO is basically a company looking for money, while a SPAC is money looking for a company."

2. A SPAC IPO is usually priced at $10 per unit. These units split after 52 days into one share and a fraction of a warrant. For example, some SPACs might give you one warrant for every three units owned.

3. The SPAC usually has two years to find an operating company to merge with. If they don't find an operating company in two years, they are expected to return the money to investors.

4. There are two strategies that can be used with SPACS, and one of them is the closest thing to a free lunch in financial markets. After an operating company is found, a vote is held of the SPAC shareholders. A SPAC shareholder can choose to vote no and get their $10 back.

They get to keep their warrants and if the business combination does well in the future, the warrants, which can be converted to shares at a predetermined price, provide upside.

5. Most SPACs tend to perform poorly post-merger. They provide fertile hunting grounds for investors that short stocks assuming the cost to borrow shares to short is not very high.

CHAPTER 6

SPINOFFS

SPINOFFS ARE PART of the circle of life for companies. When companies are young, they grow organically. When they approach middle age and organic growth slows, they instead grow through a series of acquisitions. Upon reaching maturity they start spinning off divisions of the company—jettisoning them to form new, independent companies. In some instances a company that was acquired years ago, with a lot of fanfare and expectations of synergies, is spun out because it is no longer a good fit for the wider organization.

For example, the data storage company Veritas, which was acquired by Symactec for $13.5bn in 2005, was spun out a decade later for just $8bn—sold to a group of private investors. In most cases the existing shareholders of the company receive shares of the spinoff, and there are several very successful spinoffs that in some cases eclipsed the glory of their parents. These include the spinoff of PayPal from eBay and, as discussed in Chapter 1, the spinoff of Ferrari from Fiat Chrysler (NYSE: STLA).

When companies are initially spun off from their parents, large funds and other institutional managers often do not want to keep the spinoff in their portfolio and tend to sell them shortly after.

One reason could be that the spinoff does not meet the fund's mandate. In other words, if the fund is a large-cap fund that only invests in companies that have a market cap of over $10bn, a small spinoff that is only worth $1.5bn does not meet the fund's criteria and hence has no place in the fund's portfolio.

This often leads to forced selling, and the spinoff usually sees its stock price decline for several weeks or months. Investors that focus on spinoffs are happy to swoop in and pick up some of the unfairly beaten stock. These spinoffs tend to go on to perform well, partly due to mean reversion but also because they benefit from newly incentivized management teams that are now free to grow the company or take it in new directions.

After Joel Greenblatt's book *You Can be a Stock Market Genius* shone a bright light on the potential of spinoffs, a broader swath of investors started paying attention.[19] Before long the juicy opportunities of the dark ages before his book was published had largely dried up. Nevertheless with patience in short supply on Wall Street, spinoffs do provide for fertile hunting grounds if you know where to look.

Spinoffs, carve-outs, split-offs and Reverse Morris Trusts

There are four types of spinoffs:

1. Spinoffs: In a spinoff, existing shareholders receive shares of the spinoff much like you would receive a special dividend. The 2019 spinoff of brands like Wrangler and Lee into a company called Kontoor Brands (NYSE: KTB) from its parent VF Corporation (NYSE: VFC) is an example of a spinoff.

2. split-offs: A split-off occurs when shareholders are given the option to receive shares of the subsidiary in lieu of their shares in the parent. Investors can choose to retain shares of the parent or the subsidiary but cannot keep both.

3. Carve-outs: A carve-out is a process by which a parent company sells all or some of its shares in a subsidiary in an IPO. The separation of Chipotle Mexican Grill (NYSE: CMG) from McDonald's (NYSE: MCD) was an example of a carve-out. The IPO of the dating-focused company Match Group (Nasdaq: MTCH) in November 2015 was another example of a carve-out. IAC retained nearly 85% of the class A shares after the carve-out. The two companies fully separated in mid-2020 in what was the largest business separation for IAC in its 25-year history, which included spinoffs of companies like Expedia (Nasdaq: EXPE), Ticketmaster and LendingTree (Nasdaq: TREE). Match Group, with its portfolio of properties including Tinder, had a market cap of $30bn at separation.

4. Reverse Morris Trusts: This is a tax-efficient type of spinoff where a parent company spins off a subsidiary and at the same time merges it with another company. When the pharmaceutical giant Pfizer (NYSE: PFE) wanted to separate its generic drugs business called Upjohn, it used a Reverse Morris Trust transaction by merging Upjohn with the publicly traded generic drugs company Mylan (the maker of EpiPen) in 2020. The combined company was called Viatris (VTRS).

Which should you choose? Parent or child?

For every Chipotle Mexican Grill or Otis Worldwide (NYSE: OTIS) that were successfully spun out of McDonald's and Raytheon Technologies (NYSE: RTX) respectively, there will be several other spinoffs that perform poorly. For example, while IAC has had a long history of acquiring companies, building them up and then spinning them off, they stumbled with a recent attempt. The video sharing platform Vimeo was spun out from IAC in May 2021 and went on to lose more than 90% of its value.

One of the reasons some spinoffs perform poorly is because parent companies with leveraged balance sheets often load the spinoffs with a disproportionate amount of debt. This reduces the burden on the parent, helping it report strong earnings. I have also seen situations where a retail REIT that had over 100 malls in its portfolio, including several underperforming malls in Puerto Rico, spun off its undesirable assets into a separate REIT and kept the stronger-performing malls in its portfolio.

Companies that are spinning off a division are required to file a form called the Form 10-12B with the SEC that includes important information about the parent and the spinoff, as well as pro-forma financial statements for the spinoff.

Companies often share investor presentations that can be very helpful in understanding the structure of the spinoff, the management team that will be leading the spinoff, and the opportunity the spinoff will have as an independent company.

The Form 10-12B and the investor presentations can help investors understand the motivation for the spinoff and determine whether the child company or the parent presents the more interesting opportunity for investment.

Case study 1: Pfizer, Upjohn and Mylan

Generic drugs are a blessing to consumers that cannot afford the high price of medication that is still under patent protection. This is especially true for patients in emerging market economies with very low per-capita income levels. Income per capita in India in 2020 was $1,663 for the full year. Annual per capita income in countries like Afghanistan and Madagascar was significantly lower, at $475 and $382 respectively.[20] When someone has to take care of all their needs for a full year for less than $500, it is not possible for them to shell out hundreds of dollars for expensive medication. Retirees in developed countries on a fixed income also find the constantly rising cost of drugs challenging.

What was supposed to be a panacea for consumers unfortunately turned into a vehicle for corporate greed, with the world's largest generic drug manufacturers like Teva Pharmaceuticals and Mylan conspiring with each other to raise the price of drugs that should have been available for pennies in most cases.

The public and governmental backlash against these companies reached a crescendo in 2016 on account of Mylan's egregious price increases of life-saving products like the EpiPen. When someone has a severe allergy to a particular substance, like peanuts for instance, eating food that contain peanuts can trigger a life-threatening allergic reaction called anaphylaxis that makes the body go into shock. Their blood pressure drops, and they have difficulty breathing. The use of an epinephrine injection like EpiPen can help reverse these symptoms and save lives. This is one of the reasons schools and people with severe allergies ensure they keep an EpiPen handy.

Mylan used multiple tactics to keep competitors' products off pharmacy shelves, including bribing pharmacy benefit managers (PBMs) with secret rebates, paying competitors like Teva to shelve its generic EpiPen equivalent product through favorable terms in other patent-related settlements, and using a web of exclusive agreements to keep a third competitor's products off of shelves.[21]

Once the stage was set for Mylan's illegal monopoly, the price of their EpiPens soared by 500%, from $103.50 in 2009 to over $608 in 2016. The ensuing public outrage led to congressional hearings, and Mylan's CEO was called before congress to testify.

The lawsuits that resulted from this fiasco were settled in 2022 for a combined $609m. The EpiPen situation was not the only problem facing generic drugs companies like Mylan. The entire business was in tatters after getting hit by a series of lawsuits for issues like price fixing and pushing addictive medication, as well as the financial blows from several ill-timed and expensive acquisitions that left many companies with a lot of debt on their balance sheets. Some such as Mylan saw their stocks sell off after these scandals. Their business models were broken, and investors were not sure about the extent of exposure these companies had to lawsuits.

The Reverse Morris Trust transaction through which Pfizer merged its generic drugs business Upjohn with the publicly traded generic drugs company Mylan was a way for Mylan to distance itself from these scandals and bolster itself to survive the lawsuits. I was initially interested in the spinoff because Mylan's stock was already cheap before Upjohn was merged into it.

As more details about the spinoff emerged, I realized that Pfizer intended to load the spinoff with a significant amount of debt by having Upjohn issue $12bn of debt at or prior to separation. The proceeds of this debt were going to Pfizer, leaving the spinoff with an astounding $24.5bn of total debt outstanding at the close of the transaction. This includes both the debt Mylan had on its balance sheet and the additional debt Upjohn took on to pay Pfizer.

While Mr. Greenblatt casts leveraged spinoffs with a large amount of debt in a favorable light in his book, having invested through the gut-wrenching bear markets of 2001–2003 and 2007–2009 I have a different view. I find leverage to be a significant risk, especially if the economics of the new company don't support an unusually large amount of debt. Companies with a large amount of debt are more likely to go bankrupt, especially if their fate is tied to that of the overall economy and rising interest rates.

The spinoff closed in November 2020, during the Covid-19 pandemic, and as expected the parent and child went in opposite directions. In the two years that followed, Pfizer went on to notch gains of 34%, while the child company, Viatris, dropped nearly 36%, accounting for a 70% difference in performance between the two companies as you can see in Image 6.1.

Image 6.1: Difference in performance between Viatris and Pfizer

Source: Yahoo Finance

As an investor in spinoffs, it is not just important to understand the specifics of the spinoff but also broader industry dynamics to see if there is something more going on than initially meets the eye. In the Pfizer-Upjohn-Mylan triangle, the parent, Pfizer, emerged a clear winner. Pfizer struck a deal with BioNTech to jointly develop a highly effective MRA Covid-19 vaccine.

The company used the large profits from vaccine sales to go on a buying spree and acquire several public companies to bolster its pipeline of drugs. I decided to purchase Pfizer for my portfolio based on these developments. The icing on the cake was that many of the deals Pfizer struck to acquire development-stage drug companies turned into excellent merger arbitrage opportunities that offered excellent spreads on deals that closed in very short periods of time.

Case study 2: Biohaven

The second case study I want to discuss, where the outcome was significantly more favorable for the spinoff, also has Pfizer in a starring role. As we've just seen, Pfizer used its Covid vaccine-related profit bonanza to go shopping for biotech and pharmaceutical companies that already had FDA-approved drugs or promising drugs in their pipeline.

These deals were advantageous to all parties involved as these smaller companies that Pfizer was acquiring received access to Pfizer's large marketing and distribution network, and Pfizer got to expand its portfolio through new drugs. Considering how closely Pfizer had worked with various governments to ensure the smooth rollout of the Covid-19 vaccine, I figured regulators weren't going to attempt to stop these deals, and many of them ended up closing less than three months after they were announced.

One of these mergers had an unusual structure. On May 10, 2022, Pfizer announced that it was acquiring Biohaven Pharmaceutical in an $11.6bn deal. Shareholders of Biohaven would receive $148.50 per share in cash, a hefty premium of nearly 79% to the prior day's closing price. Shareholders were probably so thrilled by this news that they didn't pay a whole lot of attention to the fact that for every two shares of Biohaven they held, they would also receive one share in a new spinoff company—often referred to as a SpinCo—after the acquisition closed.

Biohaven's stock closed at $141 shortly after the deal was announced, providing $7.50 per share in profits for a return of 5.32% to arbitrageurs. The deal closed 143 days after announcement, providing arbitrageurs like me with an annualized return of over 13%.

While many parent companies load their spinoffs with a large amount of debt, in this case the new company was supposed to be seeded with $275m in cash net of any securities or cash already held by the spinoff. The deal got even sweeter with the spinoff entitled to tiered royalty payments related to the sales of certain approved products like the leading migraine drug Nurtec ODT (rimegepant) and products like Zavzpret (zavegepant)—a nasal spray for the acute treatment of migraines—that were in the process of getting FDA approval.

Companies are required to file a form called the current report or 8-K with the SEC to announce major events that could impact shareholders, and they have to do so within four business days of the event. The specific clause related to the royalty payments outlined in the 8-K that Pfizer filed with the SEC is given below:

> SpinCo will be funded by a cash contribution immediately prior to the effective time of the Spin-Off from the Company of $275 million, less any marketable securities and cash and cash equivalents held by SpinCo. In addition, following the Effective Time, the Company will make certain tiered royalty payments at percentage rates in the low- to mid-tens to SpinCo in respect of annual net sales of rimegepant and zavegepant in the U.S. in excess $5.25 billion, subject to an annual cap on royalties of $400 million per year. Such royalty payments would be in respect of years ended on or prior to December 31, 2040.

Full-year 2021 sales of Nurtec ODT were $462.5m, with $190m of those sales coming in during Q4 2021, a 40% increase over Q3 2021. Nurtec is approved for both preventative use and for acute episodes of migraines. This preventative use could expand the adoption of the drug if patients started taking it more frequently in anticipation of a migraine attack rather than at the onset of a current episode.

Pfizer's marketing and distribution networks should further benefit Nurtec sales. Despite using Khloe Kardashian in its marketing campaign, getting from an annual run rate of $760m to beyond $5.25bn for Nurtec ODT and zavegepant was a long shot considering global sales of migraine-related drugs in 2019 were only $1.8bn. Zavegepant showed positive phase 2 and phase 3 results and Biohaven was preparing to submit a New Drug Application to the FDA in Q1 2022.

Despite a low probability of the new SpinCo benefiting from those lofty sales targets anytime soon, it added optionality to the SpinCo beyond the $275m in cash it would receive from Pfizer. SpinCo was also going to receive certain other assets and liabilities from Biohaven related to the latter's pipeline of products. Pfizer wanted to retain all the migraine-related drugs (both approved and in the pipeline) and spin off the rest into the new SpinCo.

To spice things up a little (or rather to confuse us) the new SpinCo decided to retain the Biohaven name after the Pfizer deal closed. Things started to get very interesting when Gregory Bailey, a director of Biohaven, purchased $5.63m worth of shares at an average price of $148.04 just weeks before the deal closed. The director was clearly not buying for the 46 cents that were left in the arbitrage spread but because shareholders would receive free stock in the spinoff company if the deal closed.

The "new" Biohaven closed its first day of trading as an independent public company at $6.30. In the same week CEO Vlad Coric purchased a little over $5m worth of shares. A member of the board of directors, John Childs, also joined him and purchased $2.46m worth of shares.

The company was quick to raise $302m of additional capital (before expenses) through a secondary offering priced at $10.50 per share within weeks of the spinoff. Insiders once again purchased shares in this offering, with Mr. Childs picking up $41m worth of stock and Mr. Coric participating to the tune of $9m. As you can see from Image 6.2, three other directors also bought shares, and the CEO continued buying after the secondary offering was completed on October 25, 2022.

This little stub of a spinoff is up nearly 142% as I type this in February 2023. It was a unique situation where I saw three different strategies I follow: merger arbitrage, spinoffs, and insider transactions, come together to present a very profitable opportunity.

Image 6.2: Biohaven insider purchases

Owner	Relationship	Date	Transaction	Cost	# Shares	Value($)	Total Shares	Form 4
Coric Vlad	Chief Executive Officer	Oct 31, 2022	Buy	$15.97	25,800	411,995	1,543,394	Nov 01, 2022, 07:34 AM
Coric Vlad	Chief Executive Officer	Oct 28, 2022	Buy	$14.82	100,000	1,482,420	109,565	Oct 31, 2022, 07:52 AM
Coric Vlad	Chief Executive Officer	Oct 28, 2022	Buy	$14.87	41,930	623,352	1,517,594	Oct 31, 2022, 07:52 AM
Bailey Gregory	Director	Oct 25, 2022	Buy	$10.50	200,000	2,100,000	1,507,971	Oct 26, 2022, 06:22 PM
Coric Vlad	Chief Executive Officer	Oct 25, 2022	Buy	$10.50	853,380	8,960,490	1,475,664	Oct 26, 2022, 06:22 PM
CHILDS JOHN W	Director	Oct 25, 2022	Buy	$10.50	3,900,000	40,950,000	5,691,251	Oct 26, 2022, 06:22 PM
Buten Matthew	Chief Financial Officer	Oct 25, 2022	Buy	$10.50	142,857	1,499,999	166,663	Oct 26, 2022, 06:21 PM
GREGORY JULIA P	Director	Oct 25, 2022	Buy	$10.50	9,523	99,992	25,665	Oct 26, 2022, 06:19 PM

Source: InsideArbitrage.com

Why do spinoffs work?

In the previous section we discussed two case studies, with the parent presenting the superior choice in the first instance and the spinoff a better option in the second. Beyond the forced selling by funds alluded to earlier, what are some other reasons spinoffs work?

I am once again going to lean on a scene from the movie *Ford v Ferrari* to explain why spinoffs work. The 24 hours of Le Mans race, held near the town of Le Mans in France, is not just an ordinary race to see who comes first but a grueling spectacle that lasts a full 24 hours. It is a test of both human and machine endurance as both are pushed to the brink. The first race was held over a century ago in 1923. Winning the race is considered a badge of honor for car companies that want to demonstrate that they can build cars that are not just fast but also reliable.

When Fiat acquired Ferrari after deal talks fell apart with Ford, the legendary race car builder Carroll Shelby convinced Ford's CEO Henry Ford II to build a car that could not only compete in Le Mans but could defeat Ferrari. Shelby's racing career included winning numerous races in Aston Martins, Maseratis, and Ferraris. He had also won the 1959 Le Mans in an Aston Martin. He was *Sports Illustrated* magazine's driver of the year in 1956 and 1957.

With Shelby's assistance, Ford built the GT40 supercar and ended Ferrari's dominance at Le Mans by winning four years in row from 1966 to 1969. However, the first time Ford competed in the race, in 1965, things didn't go quite so swimmingly. While Ford managed to clock 218 miles per hour (over 350 km/hour) down the Mulsanne Straight, a lot of things fell apart and they didn't win the race, which brings us back to the scene in *Ford v Ferrari* where Carroll Shelby (played by Matt Damon) walks into the Ford CEO's office.

Carroll Shelby was intent on having full control over Ford's racing program without interference from the company's management team. He explains to a very frustrated Ford CEO how, as he sat waiting in Ford's very lovely waiting room, he watched a red folder change hands four times before it made its way to Henry Ford II. He goes on to explain that that probably didn't include the 22 or so other Ford employees that poked at it before it made its way to the 19th floor. He concludes by saying that you can't win a race by committee.

Unfettered from Ford's bureaucracy, Shelby felt that he had a shot at catapulting Ford to the top of the racing world by winning the Le Mans. With the right car and the right driver, he was able to win, with unfortunate tragic consequences that you will have to watch the movie to find out about.

This is the promise and the allure of spinoffs. Free from a corporate behemoth and with ample gas in the tank (or range in its battery), these companies can significantly outperform the market after the initial forced selling has taken its course.

This is not just conjecture or anecdotal data. Numerous academic studies over the decades have shown that spinoffs outperform the overall market.

A 2021 study by Harvard University professors Bruno Sergi and James Owers, "The ongoing contributions of spin-off research and practice to understanding corporate restructuring and wealth creation: $100bn in 1 decade," looked at 249 spinoff announcements by U.S. public companies over the span of 2007–2017 and found that these companies added $100bn in incremental value.[22] They specifically state:

> The abnormal returns associated with recent spin-off divestitures are of the same order of magnitude as those from the earlier papers, showing the sustained statistical significance and new economic materiality measures.

One of the most important parts of their paper came in the statement that they are still seeing some of the effects related to spinoffs that were first discussed in foundational papers by Hite and Owers and Schipper and Smith in 1983.[23,24] They go on to say:

> Our empirical analysis found that the stellar value-creating spin-off attributes first calibrated by Owers (1982) now 4 decades ago have been maintained into the recent past as the volume of such restructuring has increased dramatically. The initial announcement effect and attractive ex-dividend abnormal returns are still present.

As I dove into some of these papers it became clear that there were other ways to derive value from spinoffs that went beyond the post-spin performance that many of us practitioners were focused on.

The potential for outperformance comes in four flavors:

Parent stock price recovery

For the parent firm right before and around the time of the spinoff. The work done by Sergi and Owers in their paper shows that in some cases, the stock price of the parent recovers completely post-spin. In other words, the spinoff almost becomes free for the shareholders of the parent.

Parental performance

Think of the spinoff of a special dividend. When a stock trading at $10 declares a special dividend of $2 per share, traders can reasonably expect that on the ex-dividend date (the date after which you are no longer entitled to the dividend), the price of the stock would drop by around $2 to $8 per share. What Sergi and Owers are alluding to, based on their own research as well as other academic papers, is that on average, the stock of a parent company spinning off a division does not drop by as much as the value of the spinoff.

The other source for outperformance of the parent's stock comes from long-term returns. This is particularly true when the parent is spinning off a less desirable division and loads the spinoff with a lot of debt, as we saw in the Pfizer-Upjohn-Mylan case study.

Long-term returns for the child

A third source of outperformance is from the long-run returns for the spinoff after initial forced selling has abated.

Parent or child acquisition

The fourth source of outperformance comes when either the parent or spinoff become potential targets for acquisition. In some cases, the parent spins off a division to set itself up as an attractive target for acquisition.

Despite the potential outperformance, it has been challenging to invest in spinoffs in recent years. The Bloomberg U.S. Spin-off Index (now called the S&P U.S. Spin-off Index) was indeed outperforming the S&P 500 until 2019. However, things changed during the Covid-19 pandemic in 2020 and 2021. The tech bubble we experienced during the pandemic made it difficult for the spinoff index to outperform the S&P 500, considering information technology is the largest sector in the S&P 500.

As that bubble continues to deflate, we are likely to start seeing spinoffs or their parents outperform the overall market.

There is a season for every strategy, and it is possible that investors have forgotten the conclusion reached by Patrick J. Cusatis et al. in their 1993 paper "Restructuring through spinoffs: The stock market evidence" that outperformance from spinoffs comes in their second year as a public company, after the storm of indiscriminate selling in the first.[25] This is along the lines of what you would expect when a new management team takes the helm of a company. It takes time to turn around a ship, and the larger the ship the longer it takes to turn around. We discuss this in more detail in our next chapter about management changes.

Spinoffs and sum-of-the-parts (SOTP) situations

Rich Howe got interested in investing at a very young age. It helped that his parents were both in the investment business. He learned from his dad, who was a large-cap-value portfolio manager, and stayed interested in investing during high school and college. He started his career in the equity research division at one of the oldest investment firms in the United States, Eaton Vance, and eventually went on to earn the Chartered Financial Analyst (CFA) designation. Like many of us in the special situations world, he was inspired by Joel Greenblatt and decided to strike out on his own by launching Stock Spinoffs Investing, a website dedicated to spinoffs.

I have followed Rich's work closely for several years and appreciate the amount of time he puts into each situation, which can be as much as 40 hours per spinoff. I reached out to him to get his thoughts on what he looks for when analyzing spinoffs, and the three most important things he considers are:

1. Historical growth in revenue and earnings. In other words he is looking for fundamentally sound companies and prefers to avoid secular losers except for quick trades. This aligns with my experience that management teams that underperform as part of a parent company continue to underperform managing the child, and if you track their forecasts from quarter to quarter you will notice a pattern of missed expectations.

2. Cost of debt. He is fine with some debt but prefers to avoid spinoffs with a lot of debt in an environment of high interest rates. It is possible that since both of us invested during the Great Recession and financial crisis of 2008–2009, we are averse to companies with highly leveraged balance sheets, unlike Mr. Greenblatt who felt that leverage helped amplify returns. For the right company in the right interest rate environment with returns well above the cost of capital, a leveraged balance sheet could work but not for most companies.

3. He also likes to focus on the company's competitive position. Is the spinoff a market share leader in its sector? A good example of this was the Ferrari spinoff from Fiat Chrysler in January 2016. The company had amazing brand recognition, was profitable with growing revenue and, as is often the case with spinoffs, did not perform well in its first year as an independent company.

Unlike the conclusion of the Cusatis paper, Rich's approach is that he wants to see that at least 50% of the shares outstanding for the spinoff *have* traded.[26] He found that the stock bottoms after 40–60% of shares have traded, and this usually takes about seven to eight trading days. You can find the total shares outstanding from the Form 10 that is filed with the SEC before the company is spun out, and you can find the volume of shares traded each day from various financial websites that include daily trading information.

One of Rich's favorite recent investments is a sum-of-the-parts (SOTP) situation. A SOTP investment is one where a company holds several businesses or divisions and the combined estimated value of all these businesses exceeds the market value of the company. For example, at one point Yahoo! not only owned its operating businesses in the U.S. across several verticals including Yahoo! finance, sports, etc. but it also held large stakes in Chinese e-commerce giant Alibaba and Yahoo! Japan. Yahoo! Japan was a joint venture between SoftBank and Yahoo!, which was listed on the Tokyo Stock Exchange. At one point, the value of these stakes combined with a conservative valuation applied to Yahoo!'s operating businesses exceeded the value the market was assigning to Yahoo!.

The SOTP situation Rich liked was the company IAC that we discussed earlier. His estimate of the value of IAC's stock was around $85 per share in early March 2023, and the stock was trading in the low $50s per share, providing more than 55% upside if the conglomerate discount could be narrowed. Back in the 1980s conglomerates were a favorite among investors. Companies went on a buying spree and collected disparate businesses under a common corporate umbrella. For example, Warren Buffett's Berkshire Hathaway is a conglomerate, holding both stakes in public companies as well as entire private businesses that range from a furniture retailer to a builder of manufactured homes.

Even though the Berkshire Hathaway businesses operate in diverse industries ranging from insurance to transportation, they are not valued at a discount because money from these businesses flows to the parent company, and Warren Buffett and Charlie Munger were good at making decisions about where this money should be reinvested. In other words they were good allocators of excess capital. The same cannot be said for conglomerates of the 1980s, many of which took on high interest debt to fuel their buying sprees. Once it became clear that there were no synergies between these businesses and the operators of these conglomerates were not the best capital allocators, most of them started trading at a discount to the value of their underlying businesses and hence the phrase conglomerate discount.

Spinoffs unlock value in SOTP situations. For a period of time investors were fascinated by SOTP situations, where you figured out the value of the various businesses a conglomerate or holding company had and determined if the sum of each of these businesses was worth significantly more than the full company. In other words the question was: were these businesses trading at a discount because they were living under a common umbrella, and was there a way to realize their full potential?

You don't hear a lot about SOTP opportunities these days because it is both difficult to come across companies that are selling at a discount to their component parts and more importantly there may not be a clear catalyst to realize value through the narrowing of that discount.

One way for holding companies to realize the untapped value in their subsidiaries is through a spinoff. Traded as a separate entity, the spinoff could escape the clutches of the conglomerate discount and, with an incentivized management team at the helm, could supercharge growth to build something meaningful.

Companies like IAC and Cannae Holdings (NYSE: CNNE) are good at buying companies, in some cases rolling them up together and then spinning them off as separate entities.

Putting together the value of the parts in a SOTP situation takes both time and a certain amount of guesswork even if you build models to determine the value of individual businesses or divisions within a company. Companies like Cannae sometimes make our lives easier. The company not only outlined what the sum-of-the-parts of its holdings worked out to in a February 2022 investor presentation but also provided an update on March 31, 2022, that showed that the company was trading at an astounding 42% discount to its net asset value (NAV) as seen in Image 6.3.

Image 6.3: Cannae sum-of-the-parts valuation

As of March 31, 2022

$'s in millions except for values per CNNE share [1]

Company	Current Ownership	Initial Year invested	Cost of Investment	Gross Fair Value ("FV") Amount [4]	Gross Fair Value ("FV") Per CNNE Share [1]	FV, Net of Fees [2] & Taxes [3] Amount [5]	FV, Net of Fees [2] & Taxes [3] Per CNNE Share [1]	Net MOIC
dun & bradstreet	88.3M shares (~20% ownership)	2019	$ 1,062.8	$ 1,546.6	$ 18.21	$ 1,375.6	$ 16.20	1.3x
CERIDIAN	8.0M shares (~5% ownership)	2007	48.5	546.9	6.44	417.7	4.92	8.6x
alight.	52.5M shares (~10% ownership)	2021	440.5	522.1	6.15	496.1	5.84	1.1x
SYSTEM1	28.4M shares (~26% ownership) + 1.2M warrants	2022	248.3	413.7	4.87	359.5	4.23	1.4x
Paysafe:	59.8M shares (~8% ownership) + 8.1M warrants	2021	519.0	209.9	2.44	274.8	3.21	0.5x
Sightline	~33% ownership interest	2021	272.0	272.0	3.20	272.0	3.20	1.0x
AMERILIFE	~20% ownership interest	2020	121.3	121.3	1.43	121.3	1.43	1.0x
Various Other Investments [6] and Adjusted Net Cash [7]	Various equity investments	Various	166.0	166.0	1.95	166.0	1.95	1.0x
TOTAL			$ 2,878.4	$ 3,798.5	$ 44.69	$ 3,483.0	$ 40.98	1.2x

Cannae's share price of $23.92 as of 03/31/2022 is a 42% discount to the intrinsic value per share

Source: Cannae investor presentation

Staying on top of SOTP situations can help event-driven investors understand what kind of spinoffs might be in the pipeline and the history of the company before it was spun out.

Spinsider: spinoffs with insider buying

Paying attention to what insiders are doing is not just good advice when analyzing companies but is especially important for spinoff situations.

Mr. Greenblatt calls insider trading the most important area of a spinoff. While he is referring to how insiders and the new management team are incentivized with stock options or RSUs, tracking their behavior once the company becomes publicly traded is also important. As we discussed in our chapter on insider transactions, company insiders have to file a Form 4 with the SEC within two business days after a purchase or a sale.

At InsideArbitrage I maintain a list of all upcoming and completed spinoffs and track the performance of both the spinoff and the parent post-spin. An important catalyst to keep track of is whether the insiders of the spinoff are buying shares on the open market with their own money. I do this in a custom screen, called the "Spinsider."

The subject of our second case study of this chapter, Biohaven, made its way into the Spinsider screen, and so did Intel's spinoff of Mobileye, the autonomous driving technology company that Intel acquired in 2017 and then spun out in 2022.

The dark side of spinoffs

Spinoffs as a group have been shown to outperform the broader market, but not every spinoff is likely to do well even if insiders are buying on the open market. I wrote about insider buying at luxury real estate company Douglas Elliman (NYSE: DOUG) several times after the company was spun out of Vector Group (NYSE: VGR) at the end of 2021. The stock closed its first day of trading over $12 per share and insiders waited until it had dipped below $6 before they started buying. The macroenvironment for real estate and especially for luxury real estate was not the best considering the stock market had already started declining and the Fed was raising rates to bring inflation under control. Not only did the company miss earnings estimates in the first two quarters of 2022, they started posting losses in the second half of the year. The losses continued in 2023 and by August 2023 it was trading a few pennies above $2, well below where the CEO, the CFO, and the COO purchased shares.

The other challenge with spinoffs is getting the timing right. The Owers paper in the 1980s suggested that you can do well with spinoffs if you purchase them in the second year after they become an independent company. This allows for all the forced selling by funds to run its course. Considering it has become significantly easier and cheaper to trade stocks since that paper was published, the timeline suggested in that paper has shrunk. Rich Howe waits until 50% of the float has traded. Other investors who follow the strategy and have done quantitative work to figure out how long they should wait, suggest the ideal timeframe is six months after the spinoff occurs.

Each spinoff situation is unique, and it pays to dive deep into them to understand them. Sometimes it is preferable to invest in the spinoff and at other times the parent is more attractive. I have done both and have at times changed my mind right before the spinoff, as more information became available.

Bringing it all together

To summarize our chapter on spinoffs:

1. Companies spin off divisions or businesses for various reasons including giving an internal management team the reigns to

independently build and grow the business. They also sometimes spin off weak businesses and load them up with debt to leave the parent corporation much stronger after the spin.

2. Spinoffs often underperform in the short term because of forced selling by funds. Investors often have a specific style or mandate they follow, and the spinoff might not fit their style or the size of the position might be too small for them to continue holding the stock of the spinoff.

3. Over the long term, spinoffs outperform the market and some studies have shown that buying a parent before the spinoff can be beneficial as the price of the parent rebounds after the spinoff, essentially making the spinoff almost free.

4. The Form 10 companies file with the SEC combined with investor presentations are a good source of information to start understanding both the parent company and the spinoff. Reviewing this information will help you understand whether you should invest in the parent or spinoff.

5. Follow the insiders of spinoffs to understand how they are incentivized by stock options or restricted stock units (RSUs) and if they are buying additional shares on the open market after the spinoff starts trading as an independent company.

CHAPTER 7

MANAGEMENT CHANGES

WARREN BUFFETT FAMOUSLY warned of the challenge faced by company management: "When a management with a reputation for brilliance tackles a business with a reputation for bad economics, it is the reputation of the business that remains intact." So much so, that he went on to say: "Finding outstanding businesses where we can invest and grow our capital is difficult and finding brilliant management is even more difficult."

This is one of the reasons Mr. Buffett stated in his 1988 Chairman's letter to Berkshire Hathaway shareholders that "In fact, when we own portions of outstanding businesses with outstanding managements, our favorite holding period is forever."[27]

In late 2010 I was in the market to buy a washing machine and dryer. After some research I settled on a pair from Best Buy (NYSE: BBY). I was a little surprised that the best combination of selection and price happened to be at Best Buy, which was a company most consumers knew as being a big-box retailer of electronic goods instead of a place where you purchased large appliances for a home.

Big-box electronics retailers had been decimated in the prior decade with large swaths of consumers checking out products at physical stores and then placing their orders on Amazon.com. The Great Recession of 2008–2009 was a death knell for some of these retailers. Best Buy's key competitor, Circuit City, declared bankruptcy in 2009 and RadioShack, which had been limping along for a few years, declared bankruptcy in 2015.

When paying for my purchase at Best Buy, I struck up a conversation with the cashier and asked him how business was going. Oddly enough he said things were going well. I went home and checked out the stock, which was trading at around $40 per share, but I didn't want exposure to a brick-and-mortar retailer that was finding it difficult to compete online. The decision to not invest in Best Buy was the right one in the short term as the stock declined for the next two years and bottomed below $12 in late 2012.

I should have continued paying attention to Best Buy because the company managed to pull off an inspiring transformation over the next nine years. The architect of this transformation was Hubert Joly, now considered one of the top 100 CEOs according to *Harvard Business Review* and one of the top 30 CEOs by *Barron's*.

During Mr. Joly's time at Best Buy, the stock rose from around $12 per share to over $120 per share: a "10-bagger," in Peter Lynch's words. As we will discuss later in this chapter, stock price is not the best metric to measure management performance. But it does not matter which metric you pick: revenue, net income, margins, return on equity, etc. all rose during his time at Best Buy.

How did Mr. Joly pull off this transformation in the highly competitive segment of retail electronics and especially with the albatross of a brick-and-mortar infrastructure around his neck?

He outlines his management philosophy in a book he wrote called *The Heart of Business: Leadership Principles for the Next Era of Capitalism* and in a *Masters in Business* podcast interview with Barry Ritholtz.[28]

Amazon's CEO Jeff Bezos had this to say about Mr. Joly and his book:

> Best Buy's turnaround under Hubert Joly's leadership was remarkable—a case study that should and will be taught in business schools around the world. Bold and thoughtful—he has a lot to teach.

It is not everyday you see a resounding public vote of confidence from the CEO of your key competitor.

Mr. Joly started his career in France with the global management consulting firm McKinsey & Company, where he spent 13 years helping companies solve problems. More importantly, he also spent that time learning from the CEOs of the companies he advised. He was getting paid while learning from the management teams of businesses across industries.

As an investor you have probably heard that you should focus on the process and not the outcomes. If your process is good and continues to improve over time, the outcomes will take care of themselves. Hubert Joly has a similar philosophy, in which he believes that the purpose of a business is not to make money. The money is an outcome of operating a business well. He goes on to explain that there are three business imperatives.

1. The people imperative: building the right team and motivating employees,

2. The business imperative: building great products and services for your customers and clients,

3. The financial imperative: making money for all stakeholders.

Excellence in the financial imperative depends on excellence in the business imperative, which in turn depends on the people imperative.

While management philosophy is all well and good, what were some of the specific steps he took to deliver the kind of results he did?

Recognizing you have a problem is half the battle. Mr. Joly realized that consumers were spending time in Best Buy stores to try out various products, talking to their store associates, and then going back home to place their orders on Amazon.com for a lower price. His solution? He empowered front-line employees to match Amazon's prices on the spot and lock in the sale while the customer was still in the store.

Most large organizations are bloated, and there is always room for improvement on the expense side. Mr. Joly turned this to his advantage by removing $2bn of costs from the organization. He then went on to implement growth and innovation initiatives, such as convincing the CEO of Samsung—over dinner—to open 1,000 Samsung outlets within Best Buy stores. Other manufacturers like HP and Google followed. His powers of persuasion and reputation were so strong that in 2018 Amazon gave Best Buy exclusive rights to sell its Fire TV platform in stores.

Mr. Joly stepped down from the CEO role at Best Buy in 2019. He continued to advise the new CEO and the board of directors for another two years. He now teaches at Harvard Business School and serves on the boards of Johnson & Johnson and Ralph Lauren.

Management's disproportionate impact on outcomes

The disproportionate impact a CEO or a management team can have on a business cannot be overstated. While it is encouraging to see an underdog make a comeback and win, companies in need of a turnaround are notorious for not turning around. The magic really starts to happen when you combine a good management team with a strong business.

Apple, Microsoft, Costco, and Danaher Corporation (NYSE: DHR) are examples of outstanding businesses that are run by brilliant management teams. However, nothing goes on forever, and change is the only constant.

Danaher, which gets its name from the tributary of a river in the state of Montana, started out as a group of manufacturing businesses in 1984. Over the years the company transformed itself through a series of acquisitions and divestitures to become a life sciences and diagnostics company. Danaher adopted the Japanese business philosophy of *kaizen*, or continuous improvement, in its early days and has since transformed it into its own Danaher Business System (DBS).

While a superior operating system for a company goes a long way to achieving success, at the end of the day it is the people that drive outcomes. Just like the leader of a country, a CEO and their team has a huge impact on the future direction of their company. Danaher's current CEO, Rainer Blair, had been with the company for over a decade when he took the top job during the depths of the Covid-19 pandemic. Matt McGrew was with the company even longer before he took the job of CFO in January 2019.

The company has an enviable gross margin of over 60%, a net margin of nearly 23%, and has more than doubled its revenue over the last five years from $15.52bn in 2017 to $31.47bn in 2022. Much of that success can also be attributed to Danaher's previous CEO Larry Culp, who has engineered a similar transformation at GE as discussed in our first case study later in this chapter.

Investors pay attention to a lot of metrics, but for some reason company management doesn't get as much attention as it deserves.

One reason for this could be the difficulty in assigning outcomes to a management team. As Jeff Bezos once mentioned, the outcome of any good quarter at Amazon was baked in three years before. At any given moment he was working on what would come to fruition three years later.

Considering the median tenure of a CEO at a public company is just under four years, and the tenure of a CFO is even shorter at 3.5 years, crediting successful outcomes or abject failures becomes challenging for investors.[29] They often resort to metrics that reflect the effectiveness of management including net margin, return on invested capital or return on equity.

In the few instances where you find yourself invested in an outstanding business with a brilliant management team, it becomes all the more important to track any changes to the management team and the reasons for executive turnover.

Founders at the helm

I like to focus on companies that still have a founder at the helm. Getting a business off the ground is incredibly difficult, scaling one is even harder, and continuing to lead the company all the way until it becomes a publicly traded entity is a very rare achievement. This is one of the reasons you find so few founders at the helm after a few years, even if the business is immensely successful.

The few that do remain at the top have to constantly reinvent themselves. Most are household names like Bill Gates, Jeff Bezos, Steve Jobs, Michael Dell, Mark Zuckerberg, Narayana Murthy, and Jack Ma. Then there are the ones that are still CEOs but not as widely known as the Zuckerbergs of this world, including Joe Kiani who founded the medical devices company Masimo (Nasdaq: MASI) in his garage in 1989 and Jeff Lawson who founded Twilio (Nasdaq: TWLO) in 2008.

I pay special attention when these founders purchase shares of their own company on the open market, considering that they have a long history with the company and a large portion of their net worth tied to it. I pay even more attention when these founders decide to step down or are forced out, as we saw with Steve Jobs at Apple in 1985.

If part of your investment thesis rests on a founder leading the company, the departure of the founder requires revisiting that thesis. Warren Buffett once again comes to mind for saying, "You should invest in a business that even a fool can run, because someday a fool will."

While there is a lot of truth in that statement, and the quality of the business is very important, in the increasingly competitive world we live in the management team and especially founders at the top can make a huge difference to the outcome of your investment.

Performance of new management at prior companies

Management teams have to present a report card to investors every three months when they release their quarterly or annual earnings. Whether fairly or unfairly the tenure of a CEO or CFO is judged by how the stock performed while they headed the company.

When I read Barton Biggs's *Hedgehogging* shortly before the Great Recession, one of the things that struck me was just how much short-term stock movement is driven by psychology rather than the intrinsic value of companies. I was already aware that fear and greed are behind short-term stock movements and irrational markets, what surprised me was the magnitude of the short-term movements Mr. Biggs attributed to investor psychology.

At any given time we can reasonably assume that anywhere from two-thirds to three-fourths of stock price movements are driven by these sentiments. I look for two or three key takeaways from each book that I read, and this was a big one for me. It has stayed with me for over 15 years, and I was able to incorporate this insight into my investment process.

Over a long period of time, a company's intrinsic value can win out over market sentiment in determining its stock price. The measurement yardstick of stock performance can grow long or short on a whim and cannot be used to measure management performance with accuracy. In the absence of a reliable yardstick, what kind of alternatives are available to us as investors?

We can look at various metrics including organic revenue growth, increase in earnings per share, the strength of the balance sheet, and so on. However, the key metrics to focus on are return on equity (ROE) and return on assets (ROA).

ROE is calculated by dividing net income by shareholder equity. You can find the net income for any given year on the company's income statement, either from a press release announcing full-year results or the 10K annual report the company has to file with the SEC.

You can find shareholder equity on the company's balance sheet. It is determined by subtracting total liabilities from total assets. In other words, once the company pays off all its obligations by tapping into the resources it already has (cash, inventory, accounts receivable, etc.), shareholder equity is what's left over.

ROE can vary by industry, and asset-heavy companies that have a lot of real estate (factories, for instance) could have lower ROE compared to asset-light companies like software companies. For example, Walmart's ROE is 14.60% while Microsoft's ROE is an impressive 39.31%. When looking at ROE, you can compare companies within the same industry. Everyone in retail knows that Costco is a very well-run retailer, and this is reflected in its current ROE of 29.47%. In contrast a retailer like Kohl's (NYSE: KSS) has a ROE of 12.25%, and the drug store chain Rite Aid (NYSE: RAD) has negative ROE because the company is unprofitable.

When I run stock screeners to identify potential investment opportunities, I tend to look for companies with a ROE of 15% or greater.

One limitation of using ROE as a metric for management effectiveness is that unforeseen events may cause fluctuations in net income from year to year. This might make the ROE look unusually low or high at different times. Looking at the trend of the ROE and understanding the underlying factors that caused the change help dispel this limitation.

ROA functions very similarly to ROE, but instead of dividing the company's net income by its shareholder equity you divide it by the company's total assets. Considering how a large number of businesses are asset-light, I find ROA less useful than ROE. Companies like the hotel chains Marriott and Hilton are asset-light because they license their brands instead of owning physical hotels. Yum! Brands, the company that owns the Pizza Hut, KFC, Taco Bell, and Habit Burger Grill brands, franchises nearly 98% of its 55,000 restaurants in more than 155 countries so is also an asset-light business.

When a new CEO joins a company, there is usually a lot of hope and excitement surrounding that event. Hope and excitement, while useful in life, are very dangerous when it comes to investing. Once you get to a stage where you start hoping for certain outcomes, your investment is likely in trouble. Expectations built on current reality or a well-thought-out model of what is to come are a different matter.

A good framework to adopt for new management is to see what their performance was at their prior company, if that information is publicly available. You could see if that company grew its revenue, managed to expand margins, allocated capital efficiently, and achieved a respectable return on equity.

Egregious compensation or well-deserved pay?

Volumes have been written about extremely high executive compensation in recent years. CEO total compensation can sometimes be hundreds of times what the median employee at the company makes and in some instances thousands of times (yes, thousands).

Are high levels of executive compensation justified? In some cases, the answer is yes. The closest analogy is to elite athletes that get paid tens or even hundreds of millions of dollars during their short sporting careers. Just like those athletes, these executives spend a large portion of their career building the skills needed to succeed at the top. Just like those athletes they need to put in long hours, well above what you would expect from most employees. And just like those athletes they need the stamina and mental fortitude to survive the rigors of their role. These roles are all-consuming, and burnout is very common. You don't get too many shots at leading a company, so in some cases the careers of these executives could be abbreviated.

There are only a few of these executives out there and they are expected to constantly perform nearly flawlessly, with high levels of energy and foresight.

The reality unfortunately is very different. Board members that are appointed by the management team and don't have the best interests of shareholders in mind, combined with the use of compensation consultants (often brought in by the CEO), have resulted in high levels of compensation transforming into egregious levels of compensation.

If you are considering investing in a company, take a few moments to pull up its proxy statement from the SEC website and specifically check out the section called the Summary Compensation Table. According to the SEC:

> The Summary Compensation Table is the cornerstone of the SEC's required disclosure on executive compensation. The Summary Compensation Table provides, in a single location, a comprehensive overview of a company's executive pay practices. It sets out the total compensation paid to the company's chief executive officer, chief financial officer and three other most highly compensated executive officers for the past three fiscal years. The Summary Compensation Table is then followed by other tables and disclosure containing more specific information on the components of compensation for the last completed fiscal year.

This disclosure includes, among other things, information about grants of stock options and stock appreciation rights, long-term incentive plan awards, pension plans; and employment contracts and related arrangements.

A stock grant or award usually vests over a period of several years. In Google's case, it is a three-year period. A third of the grant vests after the first year and then the rest vests equally every three months. The value of the grant can also go up or down based on what happens to the market price of the company's stock.

There are two lessons for investors here.

1. Always go to the source of the information (SEC filings in this case) and verify that information, especially if you are seeing outliers in the data.

2. Take the time to read the footnotes of filings or other related information to unearth additional insights.

Another useful piece of information you are likely to find in the proxy statement is the pay ratio. Starting in 2018, investors started getting a glimpse into a new pay ratio that was mandated by the SEC for companies whose fiscal year began on January 1, 2017. The pay ratio is calculated by dividing the CEO's pay by the median compensation of its employees. So for example, if a CEO is paid $10m in total in 2018 and the median employee at that company makes $100,000, then the pay ratio is 100. For Intel, CEO Pat Gelsinger's pay worked out to an astounding 1,711 times the median pay of Intel employees, which was $104,400.

In a paper "Spinning the CEO pay ratio disclosure" by Joshua White, et al., the authors discuss how companies with very high pay ratios attempt to spin things in a positive light, lest this public knowledge impact employee morale.[30] They found that "In the second year, high ratio firms are more likely to lower their reported ratio by altering the selection of their median employee."

Companies are aware of outlandish compensation structures, and instead of addressing them by altering the pay for the CEO they insert a narrative that paints their employee relations in a positive light or pick an alternative median employee that adjusts the ratio down. The implications for a company with a high ratio are not insignificant, as the authors of the paper find that:

> Firms reporting a higher ratio experience declines in employees' view of the CEO's performance and their own pay, particularly when the reported ratio is unexpectedly high. These firms also experience lower gains in employee productivity, especially in industries where employees could directly impact sales, such as those that interact frequently with customers.

The big question we as investors want to answer is whether all this compensation leads to superior stock performance. The big picture answer is no.

The Economic Policy Institute in a study conducted in 2021 found that the compensation of top CEOs from 1978 through 2020 increased by 1,322%, growing 60% faster than stock market growth during this period and well above the 18% growth a typical worker experienced.[31] A couple of things that I liked about how this study was structured was that they adjusted the compensation for inflation, and more importantly they focused on "realized" compensation. Realized compensation counts stock awards when vested and stock options when cashed in rather than when granted.

From 1978 through 2000, both granted and realized compensation tracked each other closely. After this period the correlation fell apart. Given CEO compensation in recent years has shifted more towards an outsized portion from stock awards instead of guaranteed cash compensation, this breakdown in correlation makes sense as bull and bear markets have a larger impact on CEO compensation this century than they did in the 20th century.

Now that we have understood how to find information about executive pay and how it has far outpaced the overall return of the stock market, can we infer anything about companies that overpay or underpay their CEOs? In other words if you find companies in your portfolio that are very generous with their executive compensation, do you need to take any action?

In a research paper published by MSCI, the research company looked at the relations between 10-year realized CEO total pay and 10-year total shareholder return during the 2006–2015 period, covering 423 companies.[32] They found that:

> The bottom fifth of companies by equity incentive award outperformed the top fifth by nearly 39% on average on a 10-year cumulative basis.

Not only did higher pay not translate into better performance, the impact was the exact opposite of what compensation consultants and CEOs would have us believe. The companies that paid their CEOs the least outperformed the ones that paid the most by 39%.

They attributed the underperformance of the most generous firms to short-term performance assessments, poor succession planning, SEC-mandated annual reporting standards and to an over-reliance on share price-related performance measures. As discussed earlier in this chapter, share price is not a good yardstick to measure management performance. We must look at other metrics, including ROE over long periods of time, to understand how a management team is performing.

Case study 1: Qualtrics International

In April 2022 I was looking into a company called Qualtrics International (Nasdaq: XM) that was spun off from the German software giant SAP through an IPO in 2021.

Qualtrics International helps businesses measure customer satisfaction through a system they refer to as Experience Management operating system (XMos). Over 16,000 brands and 75% of Fortune 100 companies use the Qualtrics XMos.

Qualtrics measures customer satisfaction through a single-question standardized survey called the Net Promoter Score (NPS) that was developed by Bain & Company in 2003. You may have seen this survey yourself, as it is commonly presented to customers after they engage with businesses of all types and sizes. The question asks how likely you are to recommend the company/product/service to friends and colleagues.

The response options range from 0–10. Customers responding to the survey are put into three buckets:

1. **Promoters:** These are customers who rated the business a 9 or a 10. They are very likely to recommend the business to others.

2. **Passives:** These are customers that responded with a 7 or 8. They are not likely to recommend the business to others but are likely to continue using products or services provided by the business.

3. **Detractors:** These folks were not particularly happy with the product, service, or value they received from the business and rated the survey question anywhere from 0–6.

To calculate the NPS, you discard any response that was a 7 or 8 (the passives). You then subtract the detractors from promoters. If all your respondents are promoters, you end up with a total score of 100 and everyone is happy. If all your customers are detractors then the total score works out to -100 and will likely trigger a series of urgent meetings within the organization to understand the problems and move quickly to fix them. If the business only received passive responses, then the total score would be 0. Hence the score for most companies likely falls somewhere between –100 and 100.

Some public companies have started reporting their NPS scores, and investors are using a high NPS score as a quality indicator for companies they are analyzing. I worked at a San Francisco-based company that implemented the NPS system, and the results we received were insightful. Paying attention to the responses received from a NPS system can help companies adopt a continuous improvement approach.

Getting back to Qualtrics, the company that had made a business for itself by helping companies implement NPS systems and draw insights from the results, I was struck by something I noticed on their 2021 cash flow statement.

The company had reported a net loss of $1.06bn for 2021 despite revenue growing 42% to $1.08bn. What was even more remarkable was that stock-based compensation was exactly $1.06bn. In other words, the company would have broken even had it not paid its employees with options and restricted stock units (RSUs) in 2021 to the tune of $1.06bn.

Obviously this is very simplistic thinking, and high-performing employees often have to be compensated with stock in addition to their base pay and other benefits. The larger the employee's compensation in stock, the more aligned their interests are with those of the company's shareholders. However, in the case of Qualtrics this sentiment was taken to an extreme.

Almost a year after I wrote an article about Qualtrics and its stock-based compensation, I came across the Equilar 200 study, which listed the U.S. public company CEOs with the largest total compensation for 2021.[33]

The top spot was held by the founder and CEO of advertising company The Trade Desk, with a total compensation of a whopping $835m. Founders and very early investors have a lot of their net worth tied into the company's stock, and their incentives are closely aligned with those of shareholders. The second spot on the list belonged to Zig Serafin, the CEO of Qualtrics, with total compensation of over $540m. More than half of the stock-based compensation the company reported on its cash flow statement for 2021 went to its CEO. More than half a billion dollars. $540,513,050 to be precise.

How did Qualtrics' shareholders fare? When the company was initially spun off, its IPO had been priced at $30 per share. It closed its first day of trading with a share price of $45.50 and then began a decline a few days later to end 2021 at $35.40. After the tech bubble burst in 2022, the stock finally bottomed at $9.65 in November of that year.

The Qualtrics story ended with an all-cash acquisition by the private equity firm Silver Lake and Canada's Pension Plan Investment Board (CPP Investments) in March 2023. They acquired the company for $12.5bn, or $18.15 per share, after paying a big premium of 73%. Management options and stock grants usually get accelerated in an acquisition, and they get paid out when the acquisition closes. The IPO investors and anyone that invested since the company went public were out of luck.

When I pulled up the proxy statements for Qualtrics and a few other companies, I realized that the Equilar 200 study I referenced earlier had one flaw in the way it calculated total compensation. It used the full value of a stock grant in the year it was granted instead of spreading it out over the vesting period. For example, Google CEO Sundar Pichai was awarded a stock grant worth nearly $273m in 2019 in addition to his base salary of $650,000 and other compensation of $3.36m, which put his total compensation for that year at $280.62 million. He received no additional stock grants in 2020 and 2021 and hence did not make it into Equilar's list of the top paid CEOs for 2021.

Qualtrics was not the only company that stood out in the list of top 200 CEOs with the highest pay for 2021. The 10th spot on the list was held by Intel's (Nasdaq: INTC) CEO Pat Gelsinger with a total compensation of $178m.

Mr. Gelsinger's return to Intel as CEO in February 2021 was a ray of hope for the company, which had been faltering in its core business due to competition from AMD and Nvidia. Mr. Gelsinger had recently served as CEO of server virtualization company VMware since 2012 but more importantly had previously spent 30 years at Intel in various roles that culminated in his becoming chief technology officer. He was responsible for driving the creation of technologies like USB and Wi-Fi and was the architect of the original 80486 processor.

How did Intel fare under Mr. Gelsinger? In the first two years after he took the top job, Intel saw its stock lose more than half its value compared to a loss of 18% for the Nasdaq over the same period. Turning around a company the size of Intel takes time, but we should have started seeing green shoots by the second year. As discussed earlier, using stock price to measure management performance might not be the best approach and ROE is a better yardstick. Intel saw its net profit shrink sharply from $19.87bn in 2021 to $8.01bn in 2022. ROE had dropped to just 7.9% and the company cut its dividend by 65%.

It is possible that Intel's fortunes might change in the future and, as discussed in the next case study, sometimes it can take several years to turn around a large company. The jury is still out on Intel and investors will have to wait and see if Mr. Gelsinger can pull off the same kind of transformation that Lisa Su was able to achieve at archrival AMD when she was appointed CEO in 2014.

Case study 2: General Electric

Founded in the 19th century, for well over a century General Electric (NYSE: GE) was a shining beacon of innovation and corporate leadership. The company was a crucible for management talent, and more than a dozen ex-GE managers went to lead large publicly traded companies like Albertson's and Home Depot.

The bursting of the dot-com bubble in 2000 also marked the beginning of a new chapter for GE that included multiple restatements of its financial results, probes into accounting practices at the company by the SEC, a balance sheet that was drowning in well over $200bn of net debt and a stock price that had collapsed. Stories about how GE's CEO Jeff Immelt had an empty business jet follow his corporate jet in case the first jet faced any mechanical issues further tarnished the reputation of the company.

The finance division of GE was on the verge of failing in 2008 before Warren Buffett invested $3bn, saving it from a massive meltdown. Again in 2020, GE, like all other businesses worldwide, was hit by the Covid-19 pandemic, and many areas, particularly aviation, suffered significant setbacks. After nearly two decades of mismanagement, by 2020, investors had given up on the stock of one of the most storied companies on Wall Street.

Joining GE's board of directors in April 2018, before becoming the CEO of the company in October 2018, Larry Culp has managed to engineer a big turnaround at the company. I like to say that turnaround attempts hold a lot of potential, but they rarely turn around. The larger the company and the deeper the hole, the longer it takes to engineer a turnaround. The hole was very deep at GE.

After the initial stock price spike following Mr. Culp's appointment at GE, the stock went on to drop more than 40% over the subsequent two months. For a while it looked like he had bitten off more than he could chew. Gradually under Mr. Culp's leadership, GE managed to reduce its gross debt by over $90bn, and he led the effort to refocus GE on its core businesses. He started selling divisions including its lighting and biopharma businesses, as well as spinning off GE Transportation through a merger with Wabtec in early 2019.

Mr. Culp is well known not only for his transformation of GE, but also for his transformation of Danaher, which he joined in 1990 and led as CEO from 2000 to 2014. During his time at the company, Mr. Culp raised its market cap and revenue fivefold, and built Danaher into a giant conglomerate, with over $22bn in acquisitions.

Both acquisitions and spinoffs are tools that GE has employed numerous times in the past, but under Mr. Culp's leadership, the company has focused on downsizing, especially by employing spinoffs for its various business segments.

The mantra with spinoffs is to load the spinoff with a lot of debt. GE has been following this playbook by loading its spinoffs, including GE Healthcare, with plenty. The transformation of GE is almost complete as I write this in late 2023 with almost no net debt on the balance sheet and just one more spinoff in the pipeline. GE intends to spin off its power and renewable energy business in 2024, leaving behind a lean company that focuses almost exclusively on aviation.

Both GE's management team and investors are seeing the light at the end of the tunnel. Four different insiders, including Mr. Culp, purchased shares on the open market in May 2022 and as I write this, the stock is up more than 100% over the last year, significantly outperforming the S&P 500 Index.

Mr. Culp's performance at Danaher over a long period of time was the signal for GE investors that there was a high probability of a turnaround at GE but that it would take time to reorient the ship, especially when it was hit by a storm like Covid-19 in the midst of its turnaround. The insider buying and improving health of the balance sheet were other markers along the way that pointed to a bright future.

The dark side of management changes

The two case studies discussed in this chapter show the stark contrast in outcomes at two companies under different CEOs. Tracking the performance of the CEO at a prior company, checking for egregious compensation and tracking sudden departures can help paint a picture of the potential performance of a company that has experienced management turnover. However, that in itself is not sufficient.

Marissa Mayer, the CEO of Yahoo! from 2012 to 2017 is an example of a star CEO who was brought in to transform the company. Ms. Mayer had been an executive at Google, a company she joined as only its 20th employee in 1999 right after getting her bachelor's and master's degrees from Stanford University. She was well educated, talented, had worked on numerous Google products that brought in significant revenue such as Adwords and Google Maps, and led acquisitions.

Going into her appointment in 2012, it would have been hard to imagine that she would face calls for her replacement by several hedge funds less than three years later. She presided over the $1.1bn acquisition of Tumblr in 2013, which was eventually sold by Yahoo! in 2019 for just $3m. She sold part of Yahoo!'s valuable stake in Chinese e-commerce giant Alibaba back to Alibaba in a transaction that in her own words eroded "tens of billions of dollars of upside."[34] She oversaw a huge reduction in advertising revenue by the time she agreed to step down as CEO in 2017. This was partially the case of a bad business meeting good management and the reputation of the business surviving the ordeal.

If the new CEO's track record at a prior company is not enough to guide you as an investor, what is? Just as I discussed in our chapters on insider transactions, stock buybacks and spinoffs, the answer is more nuanced and requires looking at a mosaic of information including whether the insiders are buying stock with their own money or quickly cashing in their generous stock-based compensation, are the company's financials reflecting the CEO's optimism and is the company executing an optimal capital allocation strategy whether it is through thoughtful acquisitions or spinning off divisions.

Michelle Leder is a financial journalist and the author of the book *Financial Fine Print: Uncovering a Company's True Value*.[35] After getting burnt by an investment early in her investing journey, much like I was, she started digging deep into the footnotes of SEC filings for insights. As she outlines in her book, the former chairman of the SEC once remarked,

Too many companies would prefer that you not read the footnotes. That should be incentive enough to delve into them.

Insights gleaned from the fine print or the footnotes of SEC filings like a company's annual report (10K) and quarterly reports (10Q) combined with information in the 8-K can help you uncover issues with a company long before you see it in the financial media or on TV. Subtle changes to the footnotes from one quarter to the next or a change in the language in the "risk factors" section of the filings can warn investors that the company might be at risk of bankruptcy.

The information that can be unearthed by paying close attention to the filings is not always bad and, in some cases can signal that the company might be the target of an acquisition.

A section of the 8-K that I pay special attention to is "Item 5.02" that announces departures from the company's management team, election of directors, appointment of new officers, and compensation paid to certain members of the management team.

For example, when Netflix's founder, Reed Hastings, decided to resign from his role of co-CEO, the company reported the following in an 8-K filed with the SEC on January 19, 2023:

Item 5.02 Departure of Directors or Certain Officers; Election of Directors; Appointment of Certain Officers; Compensatory Arrangements of Certain Officers.

On January 13, 2023, Reed Hastings was appointed as Executive Chairman of the Board of directors (the "Board") of the Company, effective immediately. At that time, Mr. Hastings resigned his role as co-Chief Executive Officer and President of the Company, but remains an employee of the Company in his new role as Executive Chairman. Also on January 13, 2023, Greg Peters, age 52, was appointed as co-Chief Executive Officer of the Company. Mr. Peters will serve as co-Chief Executive Officer with Ted Sarandos, the Company's co-Chief Executive Officer. Additionally, Mr. Peters has been appointed to the Board and will hold office as a Class I director. He has not yet been appointed to serve as a member of any Board committee. Both appointments were effective as of January 13, 2023.

Mr. Hastings' transition was likely planned for a long time, and he will continue to remain involved with Netflix in the position of executive chairman, much like Jeff Bezos at Amazon.

Ms. Leder mentioned in an interview that the biggest red flag she looks for in SEC filings is sudden resignations. Bad news such as the departure of an executive is often disclosed after the market closes on a Friday or right before a three-day holiday weekend, when most analysts and market participants are not paying attention. This is one of the reasons I track sudden departures separately when I report on C-suite transitions every week.

If a company executive with a wealth of knowledge about how a company operates, and who is likely involved in projects that are critical to the success of a company, decides to depart suddenly for unspecified reasons it could point to deeper issues at the company. This is one of the reasons some companies go out of their way to indicate that the departure had nothing to do with financial reporting or other issues at the company.

In one rather amusing instance, there was a departure at a software security company where the executive took a sabbatical after working for 15 years at the company. While reporting on her subsequent departure from the company, the company indicated that the executive enjoyed traveling and cycling so much that she decided to not return to work. Glancing at her LinkedIn profile, it appears that she is still on sabbatical as of this writing.

When Vista Outdoor (NYSE: VSTO), a company that sells outdoor sports equipment and ammunition, announced that the board of directors had asked the company's CEO, Chris Metz, to resign from his position, it specifically went on to say:

> On February 2, 2023, the Board of directors of Vista Outdoor Inc. ("Vista Outdoor" or the "Company") announced that Christopher T. Metz has resigned, effective as of February 1, 2023, from his position as Chief Executive Officer and as a director of the Company at the request of the Board based on the Board's loss of confidence in his leadership *for reasons not involving financial reporting or internal controls.*[36]

If you continued following management changes at the company, you would have noticed that just two weeks later, the general counsel of the company, Dylan Ramsey, also resigned.

Vista Outdoor was attempting to split the company by spinning off its outdoor products division that included popular brands like CamelBak, Bell, and Bushnell. The remaining sporting products division that designs, manufactures, and distributes ammunition parts for the military, law enforcement, and hunters would remain with the parent company. Mr. Metz was supposed to lead the new outdoor products company as its CEO.

Clearly something related to the spinoff appears to have gone off the rails, which triggered the departure of these two executives. Just months before these departures, in October 2022, the CFO had decided to leave to pursue other opportunities.

Individual people on the management team might resign for all sorts of reasons, but you need to pay special attention when a cluster of insiders leave or the CEO's office ends up with a revolving door.

Sudden departures and rapid churn, where management team members only last a few months, are strong sell signals for long investors who already own the company's stock. They are also used as signals by short sellers who are looking to short companies that have problems underneath the surface.

Bringing it all together

To summarize our chapter on management changes:

1. Management changes can have a disproportionate impact on the future trajectory of a company.

2. If your investment thesis relies on a founder at the helm, pay attention to the founder stepping down, especially if they don't remain involved in a different role such as the executive chair of the board.

3. Sudden departures are considered a red flag, and short sellers often track them to see if there are underlying issues with a company. Sudden departures happen surprisingly often at public companies. If you notice multiple sudden departures at a company, or if the reasons provided for the sudden departure don't sound convincing, take a deeper look at what is going on at the company.

4. Measure management performance using the right yardsticks like return on equity (ROE) or margin expansion instead of stock performance over short periods of time. Management performance at a prior company could be indicative of how they are likely to perform in their new home.

5. Excessive CEO compensation can be demoralizing to a company's employees. Compensation information and the pay ratio, comparing the CEO's pay to the pay of a median employee at the company, can be found in the company's proxy statement filed with the SEC. Companies with excessive CEO pay have been shown to underperform companies with lower levels of CEO pay.

CONCLUSION

THE GREEK PHILOSOPHER Heraclitus is credited with saying that the only constant in life is change. Nowhere is this more true than financial markets. Deep involvement with financial markets entails a lifelong commitment to learning. New companies, entirely new industries, and emerging markets require you to learn new things, expand your mental models and sometimes relearn the lessons of the past.

Another aspect of markets is that they move in cycles, and the more things change the more they stay the same. I have specific volatility-related trades that I only get a chance to put on once a decade or less. The Sergi and Owers study referenced in the chapter on spinoffs was remarkable because it showed that some of the effects related to spinoffs that were observed nearly four decades earlier continued to persist. I see the same thing with strategies like merger arbitrage, where practitioners of the strategy continue to use it decade after decade.

Event-driven strategies sometimes allow you to see patterns that draw your attention to companies that may otherwise not have been on your radar. The various strategies discussed in this book are an amazing engine for idea generation, but there is no substitute for deep due diligence in determining which ideas are worthy of investment, which ones need to be added to a watchlist for further monitoring and which ones go straight to the rejection pile.

I hope you have enjoyed reading this book and that you will benefit from exploring event-driven strategies, either as countercyclical alternatives for your portfolio or to inform your idea-discovery process.

ACKNOWLEDGMENTS

This project started its life as six Twitter threads, one for each strategy discussed in this book. I want to thank Craig Pearce for championing this book internally at Harriman House and guiding me through the chapter on insider transactions. I would have never connected with Craig without warm introductions from both Vitaliy Katsenelson and Tobias Carlisle, and I am thankful for their generosity. I want to thank my editor Nick Fletcher who was instrumental in helping me become a better author and transforming this book into its current format.

I want to thank my early reviewers including my wife, my daughters, Dr. Joshua White at Vanderbilt University, Brian Stark and Shravan Paul. I want to thank Jesse Felder for reading an early version of this book and inviting me on his podcast for a wonderful conversation in Silicon Valley.

I want to thank David Jackson for allowing me to become an early contributor on Seeking Alpha in 2005 and giving me a platform to share my investment research with the broader investment community. Dave Callaway was instrumental in providing early feedback to me in the mid-2000s and helping me understand the difference between writing as an analyst and a storyteller. I want to thank Jeff Nibler, Paul Goodrich and Brad Hummel for their friendship, guidance and good counsel during key moments in my career. Above all I want to thank my parents for bringing me into this world, providing for our family and giving me the opportunities to explore my passions.

NOTES

1 Biggs, B., *Hedgehogging* (Wiley, 2008).

2 Thorndike, W., *The Outsiders* (Harvard, 2012).

3 Frenkel, S., "What Are Spam Bots and Why They're an Issue in Elon Musk's Twitter Deal" (*New York Times*, July 11, 2022). Retrieved from: www.nytimes.com/2022/07/09/technology/elon-musk-twitter-spam-bots.html#:~:text=Since%20it%20went%20public%20in,can%20pass%20anti-spam%20tests.

4 Greenblatt, J., *You Can Be a Stock Market Genius* (Simon and Schuster, 1997).

5 Leonard, J., et al. "China's Apple iPhone Ban Appears to Be Retaliation, US Says" (*Bloomberg UK*, September 13, 2023). Retrieved from www.bloomberg.com/news/articles/2023-09-13/china-s-apple-iphone-ban-appears-to-be-retaliation-us-says.

6 Mitchell, M. and Pulvino, T., "Characteristics of Risk and Return in Risk Arbitrage" (*Journal of Finance*, October 2000). Retrieved from papers.ssrn.com/sol3/papers.cfm?abstract_id=268144.

7 Dieudonné, S., Bouacha, S. and Cretin, F., "Macroeconomic Drivers Behind Risk Arbitrage Strategy" (October 1, 2020). Retrieved from papers.ssrn.com/sol3/papers.cfm?abstract_id=1705548.

8 United States Securities and Exchange Commission, EDGAR Full Text Search: www.sec.gov/edgar/search/#/category=form-cat9.

9 Bank of America, "Bank of America Corporation Announces Cash Tender Offers by BofA Securities, Inc. for up to $1.5 Billion in Aggregate Liquidation Preference of Certain Outstanding Depositary Shares of Bank of America" (November 10, 2022). Retrieved from newsroom. bankofamerica.com/content/newsroom/press-releases/2022/11/bank-of-america-corporation-announces-cash-tender-offers-by-bofa.html.

10 Einhorn, D., Sohn Investment Conference slides. Retrieved from www.10xebitda.com/wp-content/uploads/2016/11/Greenlight-Pioneer-Presentation-May-2015.pdf.

11 Einhorn, D., *Fooling Some of the People All of the Time, A Long Short (and Now Complete) Story* (Wiley, 2011).

12 Pabrai, M., "Move Over Small Dogs Of The Dow, Here Come The Uber Cannibals" (Forbes, December 26, 2016). Retrieved from www. forbes.com/sites/janetnovack/2016/12/22/move-over-small-dogs-of-the-dow-here-come-the-uber-cannibals/?sh=44ed7b5c7f92.

13 United States Securities and Exchange Commission, Form 10-Q. Retrieved from www.sec.gov/ix?doc=/Archives/edgar/data/723612/000072361220000057/car-2020033110q.htm.

14 Ikenberry, D., Lakonishok, J. and Vermaelen, T., "Market Underreaction to Open Market Share Repurchases" (*Journal of Financial Economics*, 29,2–3). Retrieved from www.sciencedirect.com/science/article/abs/pii/0304405X9500826Z.

15 Chan, K., Ikenberry, D., Lee, I. and Wang, Y., "Share Repurchases as a Potential Tool to Mislead Investors" (*Journal of Corporate Finance*, 16, 2). Retrieved from papers.ssrn.com/sol3/papers.cfm?abstract_id=1485583.

16 Hutton, A., Lee, L. and Shu, S., "Do Managers Always Know Better? Relative Accuracy of Management and Analyst Forecasts" (*Journal of Accounting Research*, April 29, 2012). Retrieved from papers.ssrn.com/sol3/papers.cfm?abstract_id=2047107.

17 Lazonick, W., "Profits Without Prosperity" (*Harvard Business Review*, September 2014). Retrieved from lazonick14.pdf (free.fr).

18 Greenspan, R., "Money for Nothing, Share for Free: A Brief History of the SPAC" (May 1, 2021). Retrieved from papers.ssrn.com/sol3/papers.cfm?abstract_id=3832710.

19 Greenblatt, J., *You Can Be a Stock Market Genius* (Simon & Schuster, 1997).

20 The World Bank, "Adjusted Net National Income Per Capita (Current US$)". Retrieved from data.worldbank.org/indicator/NY.ADJ.NNTY.PC.CD.

21 Leonard, M., "Mylan $264 Million EpiPen Price-Gouge Deal Gets First Court Nod" (*Bloomberg Law*, March 14, 2022). Retrieved from news.bloomberglaw.com/antitrust/mylan-264-million-epipen-price-gouge-deal-gets-first-court-nod.

22 Owers, J. and Sergi, B., "The Ongoing Contributions of Spin-off Research and Practice to Understanding Corporate Restructuring and Wealth Creation: $100 Billion in 1 Decade" (*Humanities & Social Sciences Communications*, June 03, 2021). Retrieved from www.nature.com/articles/s41599-021-00807-9.

23 Hite, G. and Owers, J. "Security Price Reactions around Corporate Spin Off Announcements" *Journal of Financial Economics*, 12, 409–436). Retrieved from www.sciencedirect.com/science/article/abs/pii/0304405X83900429.

24 Schipper K. and Smith, A. "Effects of Recontracting on Shareholder Wealth: The Case of Voluntary Spin Offs" (*Journal of Financial Economics*

12, 437–467). Retrieved from www.sciencedirect.com/science/article/abs/pii/0304405X83900430.

25 Cusatis, P., Miles, J. and Woolridge, J., "Restructuring Through Spinoffs: The Stock Market Evidence" (*Journal of Financial Economics*, 33–3). Retrieved from www.sciencedirect.com/science/article/abs/pii/0304405X9390009Z?via%3Dihub.

26 Ibid.

27 Berkshire Hathaway, Inc. Retrieved from www.berkshirehathaway.com/letters/1988.html.

28 Ritholtz, B., "Transcript: Hubert Joly" Retrieved from ritholtz.com/2021/09/transcript-hubert-joly.

29 Datarails, "CFOs and the C-Suite: Staying Power, Pay and Pain Points" Retrieved from www.datarails.com/research/cfostayingpower.

30 Boone, A., Starkweather, A. and White, T., "The Saliency of the CEO Pay Ratio" (*Review of Finance*, November 11, 2019). Retrieved from papers.ssrn.com/sol3/papers.cfm?abstract_id=3481540.

31 Mishel, L. and Kandra, J., "CEO Pay has Skyrocketed 1,322% Since 1978" (Economic Policy Institute, August 109, 2021). Retrieved from www.epi.org/publication/ceo-pay-in-2020/#:~:text=From%201978%20to%202020%2C%20CEO,18.0%25%20from%201978%20to%202020.

32 MSCI, "Out of Whack: U.S. CEO Pay and Long-term Investment Returns" Retrieved from www.msci.com/ceo-pay.

33 Batish, A, "New York Times 200 Highest-Paid CEOs" (Equilar, June 25, 2022). Retrieved from www.equilar.com/reports/95-equilar-new-york-times-top-200-highest-paid-ceos-2022..

34 Oreskovic, A., "Marissa Mayer Blames Short Sighted Activist Investors for Causing Yahoo to Lose Out on Tens of Billions of Dollars of Upside by Selling Alibaba Stake" (*Insider*, April 18, 2018). Retrieved from www.

businessinsider.com/marissa-mayer-blames-activist-investors-selling-yahoo-alibaba-stake-2018-4

35 Leder, M., *Financial Fine Print: Uncovering a Company's True Value* (Wiley, 2003).

36 United States Securities and Exchange Commission, Form 9-K. Retrieved from www.sec.gov/ix?doc=/Archives/edgar/data/1616318/000095015723000069/form8-k.htm.

ABOUT THE AUTHOR

Asif Suria is an entrepreneur and investor with a focus on event-driven strategies including merger arbitrage, spinoffs, (legal) insider trading, buybacks, and SPACs. He was one of the earliest contributors to Seeking Alpha in 2005, and his work has been mentioned in Barron's, Dow Jones, BNN Bloomberg, and other publications.

He has been an active investor for more than two decades, and his background in technology has helped him build tools that inform his investing process, especially as it relates to event-driven strategies that require updated data and processes. He previously ran a quantitative investment firm focused on insider transactions.

Operating experience as an executive at venture-funded San Francisco Bay Area-based companies gave him a front-row seat to understanding how to build and grow companies.